# Making Sense of Religion

# Making Sense of Religion

A Study of World Religions and Theology

RICHARD L. CORLISS

Foreword by
David Boyer

WIPF & STOCK · Eugene, Oregon

MAKING SENSE OF RELIGION
A Study of World Religions and Theology

Copyright © 2014 Richard L. Corliss. All rights reserved. Except for brief quotations in critical publications or reviews, no part of this book may be reproduced in any manner without prior written permission from the publisher. Write: Permissions, Wipf and Stock Publishers, 199 W. 8th Ave., Suite 3, Eugene, OR 97401.

Wipf & Stock
An Imprint of Wipf and Stock Publishers
199 W. 8th Ave., Suite 3
Eugene, OR 97401

www.wipfandstock.com

ISBN 13: 978-1-4982-0070-7

Manufactured in the U.S.A.

In memory of my wife, Mary Corliss, who made my career in philosophy possible

# Contents

*Foreword by David Boyer* | IX
*Preface* | XV
*Acknowledgments* | XVII
*Introduction* | XIX

**Part One: What Is a Religious View of Life?**

1. The Liberal Perspective | 3
2. The Conservative Perspective | 11
3. A Wittgensteinian Perspective | 20

**Part Two: A Defense**

4. Early Hinduism | 33
5. Early Buddhism | 44
6. Biblical Judaism: The Torah | 52
7. Biblical Judaism: Amos and the Prophets | 64
8. Early Christianity: Paul and the Book of Acts | 72
9. Early Christianity: The Synoptic Gospels | 90

**Part Three: Criticisms**

10. Christology | 109
11. Zen Buddhism | 124

**Part Four: Theological Issues**

12. O. Hobart Mowrer | 139
13. John Bradshaw | 160
14. Walter Rauschenbusch | 168
15. Reinhold Niebuhr | 183

*Bibliography* | 191

# Foreword

THIS SUCCINCT VOLUME PRESENTS an innovative vision of the nature of religion in its kaleidoscopic manifestations. Here I'll point up the book's value in several aspects: as presenting a definition of religion, as a sampling of some prominent world religions, as an analytical framework, as a sustained argument for its theory of religion, as a teaching tool when coupled with a reader or a survey of religions, as scholarship, and as a rational way to form preferences that can make a difference to one's own religious beliefs about life.

(Full disclosure: Dick Corliss and I were colleagues in philosophy at St. Cloud State University in Minnesota. Through the years his insights repeatedly changed my thinking about the nature of religion. This foreword is based in part on correspondence and an informal interview with the author, but always on the book unless noted.)

*Making Sense of Religion* is remarkably informative about a range of religious thinkers. Near the outset, the author's summaries and criticisms of important medieval and modern, liberal and conservative theologians triangulate his own perspective. Although his outlook is liberal broadly speaking, he distances himself from classical religious liberalism (nineteenth century onward).

It will be easier to see why if we peek ahead at his analytical theory. This book is most fundamentally about the nature of religion. To Corliss a religious view of life is the central feature that defines what it is to be a religion. The structure of a religious view of life comprises its "beliefs and assumptions about: (1) values, (2) happiness, (3) human nature, (4) rituals, (5) authority, and (6) God, the gods, Nirvana, Brahman, the Buddha-Body, Allah, and 'things' of this type." These beliefs and assumptions he calls the elements of religion, and they interact with one another as a religious tradition evolves. (Just to be clear, his six elements of a religious view of life are not values, happiness, human nature, rituals, etc., but rather *beliefs and assumptions* about each of these.)

Element two consists of beliefs and assumptions about happiness. These include "if . . . then» beliefs about achieving happiness which Corliss calls «spiritual hypotheticals.» He explains, «By happiness is meant views of wherein lies the happiness and well-being of the individual person as well as society. It also refers to [what he elsewhere calls ‹negative views› as to] wherein the spiritual death of individuals and societies lie.» His term «spiritual» is not meant to imply anything otherworldly, only that these hypotheticals are focused on type six entities. These hypotheticals also assume some view of type three, about human nature. Examples of this interplay run throughout the text. Beliefs about rituals and authority (elements four and five) are less important, but their importance can vary as a religion evolves.

In element six he stays with the list formulation I quoted throughout the book, but in conversation he uses «the Ultimate» as an umbrella concept for the «›things› of this type» in the book. If you›ve ever tried to define element six, which so many summaries of various faiths present as the single defining feature of religion or a religion, you›ve experienced how elusive it is. As his scare quotes suggest, even the word «things» can be problematic. Nirvana is certainly not a thing; theists would find it odd to refer to God as a thing; and in Mahayana metaphysics a human individual, even one well on its way to Buddhahood—a bodhisattva, for example—is not essentially a thing, only an impermanent composite with relative existence. The Tao, so variously interpretable, is not apt to come out as an entity on anyone›s reckoning. So Corliss's list formulation actually serves well in his text. Its open-ended formulation suggests the radical openness of conceptions of the Ultimate.

As to liberalism and conservatism, let me start with the contrast between elements one, beliefs about values; and two, beliefs about happiness. They bring out differences among religious views of life as to their emphases, for example happiness or bliss vs. justice. Liberals, notably John Hick, tend to underplay justice. If Hick were to take better account of the prophet Amos, he would need to restore an emphasis on the justice-seeking aspect of God›s nature. The book implies a similar dependent variability in element three, assumptions and beliefs about human nature. The world of the classical liberal is «too rosy» for a realistic portrait of us and our world.

## Foreword

Liberal theologians have tended to assume that people experience a single core Ultimate through any religion, but in different ways based on the enveloping culture. This Ultimate then gets conceptualized differently through each cultural lens. (I might add that the Western liberals Corliss reviews hear an echoing message from, for example, the Hindu interpreter Radhakrishnan, whose idea is in turn based on classical Hindu views, for example, in the *Gita*. So the historical give and take over one Ultimate appearing many ways works out very differently in India than in Western theism.)

Corliss disagrees fundamentally with these Western liberals' very conception of religion. His analysis in terms of the six elements of religion is his alternative. Without denying the relevance of evolving culture, Corliss's analysis brings out the ways that a given constellation of the six elements of religion adjusts internally, so that, for instance, the kind of god or gods that may appear in a religious view is driven by its value elements. Thus he faults, for example, Hick as inattentive to the variable texture and structure of religion.

Classical liberalism, he says, is based on religious experience. This can downplay a standard of truth and realism in religious theory. Certainly experience is important to religious life; in fact, part of Corliss's preferred standard of truth—including moral realism—is that religions need to accommodate our experiences and be realistic about what really does promote happiness (tranquility, etc.) and moral value in us.

For all that he corrects excesses of classical liberals, he distances himself much further from theologians he terms conservative, by which he means exclusionist (thinking that their religion is the only right one) and authoritarian (thinking that all their religion's canonical texts are factually true once properly understood).

Next he demonstrates how his method works by looking up close at four religious traditions through the centuries and around the world: early Hinduism, early Buddhism, Biblical Judaism and early Christianity. His method points up dramatic shifts in outlook in each of these traditions over periods of hundreds of years, and brings into focus the unique internal structure of each religious view of life at a specific stage in its evolution. The mutual adjustments among their ideas about values, happiness and the other elements are driven by internal consistency and are reminiscent, I think, of the method of reflective equilibrium in ethics. In fact moral evolution figures prominently in Corliss's portrayals of specific traditions. He notes, "This involves being aware of different moral points of view. This is what ethical theory is all about."

Here we see a developing arc of argument that will carry through the book. Corliss's selection of six elements, together with his commonsense factual and moral realism, positions him in the theological landscape. He then shows how this analytical toolkit works on a globally inclusive range of religious traditions, studying each of them at stopping points along their evolutionary tracks. This demonstration he calls "a defense."

The text thus pointedly avoids two defects that infected so much of what passed for philosophy of religion up to the late twentieth century. One of those defects is a preoccupation with provability, particularly of the basic tenets of theism. *Making Sense of Religion* thereby sidesteps much trench warfare that is irrelevant to understanding what religion is, always the most basic question in the philosophy of anything. And part of Corliss's agenda is to demonstrate, in several of the six elements, that Enlightenment critics of religion still seek to undermine a viewpoint on life that shares their own deepest values.

The other defect is a neglect of religious diversity. Only recently—under the influence of experimental, then increasingly sophisticated textbooks on "non-Western philosophy," and based on a growing popularity of scholarly comparative religion—have philosophers begun to do better at inclusion. As Corliss reminds us, Hick's first edition of *Philosophy of Religion* in the Foundations of Philosophy series at first focused on theism; to his credit the second edition was revised to include interfaith pluralism, hearing, Hick said, genuine voices in other traditions. (But see the caveats above as to Hick's understanding of these voices.)

Next we get to a defense of a more partisan kind. One anticipated criticism of his method might come from systems derived logically from canonical texts—specifically "deductive" Christologies. He profiles types of Christologies and their influential proponents. He contrasts Aquinas's and Karl Barth's conservative approaches with the historically critical methods of Albert Schweitzer and Bart Ehrman, concluding, "If some of the gospels emphasize reason and argument, it would be odd to focus exclusively on authority." Barth, he says, relies on "a conservative view of the divine command theory." Corliss warns of the potential for untrammeled fanaticism and reminds us of the conflicting views of Christ's nature, ideas, and character even within the gospels. An "inductive" approach to Christology, which evaluates the symbolic and moral weight of Christ's character vis-à-vis

## Foreword

human needs, is more "compatible with the view of religion presented in this book" than one deduced rigidly from the canonical texts about Jesus. Citing again the prophet Amos, the author prefers to place weight on biblical passages in which Jesus follows God's will "because God embodies the most important moral principles such as goodness, righteousness, and justice." Corliss thus presumes that we bring an independent moral sense to our religious experience.

He thereby not only advances his argument by meeting a specific objection, but also by showing how his method can make a difference: it can lead us to prefer one belief set over another (e.g., a view about Christ's life and his relevance to ours) as one part of a religious view of life. To this he adds a defense against a Zen-based objection that words can't help us understand a tradition that regards words, words, words as one of the enemies of enlightenment.

The book ends with an inventive view of what theology can be, in contrast, for example, to Western Christianity's cerebral systematization of its own chief tenets of faith. Corliss takes the reader to four sources that may be unfamiliar to scholars in both biblical studies and comparative religion. Two are therapists: O. Hobart Mowrer (1907–1985) and the popular John Bradshaw (1933–). Two are social critics and reformers: Walter Rauschenbusch (1861–1918) and Reinhold Niebuhr (1892–1971). All four place their theories in a religious context. As always, Corliss traces their influences, sets them off against competing views, then pointedly summarizes and critiques their pivotal views.

But his main agenda here is to show how one can adjust, as above, the interlinked components of one's own faith so as to both connect with tradition and advance human good. He thereby proposes a novel undergirding for reform theology. Note that the intended social emendations would serve justice, not in a punitive sense, but in the sense of improving distributive and institutional justice, partly as to civil rights and populism and partly as to quality of life.

Here is the end point of that arc of argument that began with a genial, inclusive understanding of religious views of life and their centrality to the nature of religion, continued with demonstrations of the workability of an analytical framework, then defended against obvious critics and has now ended with applications to one's own religious view of life—a rational basis for taking sides where it makes a difference.

*Making Sense of Religion* would work well as a textbook in beginning and advanced classes in the philosophy of religion, the Bible, Eastern religions, any specific religion or a world survey. It is not designed as a source reader or a history of religions. It will work well as a reading preview and framework for students' further readings and projects. A student might, for example, document via primary texts one of Corliss's portrayals of the six elements of religion at work in a specific religious tradition, or apply his structural analysis to fresh material.

This work distills the author's expert viewpoint, tracing back to his seminary education and a career of teaching and research. Even if students end up disagreeing with some of his argumentative points, their attention to religion and religions will be heightened and focused in ways they will always carry with them.

David Boyer
Prof. Emeritus of Philosophy
St. Cloud State University

# Preface

IN 1957, AFTER GRADUATING from Northern Baptist Seminary, I entered the graduate program in philosophy at the University of Illinois at Urbana. That was a unique year for me. The Philosophy Department had a new chair and the focus in the department was going to be on analytic philosophy and philosophy of language. Wittgenstein's *Philosophical Investigations*, his most important work, had recently been published. It was my good fortune to have a class based on that book in my first year. I took to it like a duck takes to water. My undergraduate work in philosophy led me to embrace empiricism and skepticism—a religious skeptic, but nevertheless a skeptic. Seminary did not change this. Wittgenstein's *Investigations* functioned as an antidote.

Empirical skepticisms leads one to look at oneself as living in something like a black box with shadows on a wall. The philosophical problem is how one is supposed to know what is on the outside making those shadows appear. Wittgenstein's philosophy leads one to recognize that we learn a language from a community via which we are tied together. We are not isolated things, but members of communities with which we share a language, a life, and a culture.

The concern of Wittgenstein was to understand language in general, how it functions, but also to seek to understand how it functions in the various spheres of life—science, ethics, esthetics, law, mathematics, and, of course, religion. Being a religious animal, I came to realize that I had a job to do. This book is my latest venture in carrying out that job.

# Acknowledgments

A NUMBER OF INDIVIDUALS have played a role in shaping this manuscript. There has been a Sunday morning discussion group that has been particularly helpful. That included Myron Anderson, James Lundquist, James White, and George Yoos. In addition, Patrick Henry has made criticisms that have been very helpful.

# Introduction

## THE PROJECT OF THIS BOOK

Is it possible to make sense of the multiplicity of religious views of life? By "make sense" I mean to shed light on the kind of thing found in religious views of life.

The answer to that question in this book is "yes." Religious views of life have a certain underlying logic. There are types of reasons and a type of rationality that distinguishes religion from science and ethics.

Philosophers in the tradition of Ludwig Wittgenstein consider it a role of philosophy to understand the nature of ethics, esthetics, logic, law, mathematics, science, and, of course, religion. This book is written from that point of view. The project of the book is to do three things: (1) to explicate the kinds of beliefs and assumptions that are important to religious views of life, (2) to defend that explication by examining various religious traditions and their scriptures, and (3) to show how theology can be done by making use of this view of religion to critique some religious perspectives.

The argument will be that people's beliefs and assumptions function like pieces in a puzzle which fit together to form a coherent whole. People with different religious orientations have different beliefs and assumptions which they consider important. Understanding and comparing these differences is important. Understanding these differences and their justifications is referred to in this book as theology. Not all religious orientations have what is considered a theology—for example, Zen Buddhism and Theravada Buddhism. In this book, however, discussing various religious beliefs, their differences and their rationale is referred to as theology.

To put the substance of this book in its historic context, it is important to be aware of two alternative ways of viewing religion. There is a liberal tradition which sees the roots of religion lie in religious experiences. According to this tradition religious experiences affect people's lives and beliefs, but their religious beliefs are also shaped very much by their culture. People in the various religious traditions experience the same religious ultimate. Their beliefs differ, however, because those beliefs are shaped not just by their religious experiences but by their culture.

The most influential figures in this tradition have been Frederick Schleiermacher (1768–1834), Paul Tillich (1886–1965), and John Hick. The latter was born in 1922 and is still active today. Schleiermacher became known as the father of modern theology. Paul Tillich was the most influential philosophical theologian of the mid-twentieth century. John Hick played that role in the last part of the twentieth century and continues to play that that role today. In order to understand this tradition, a brief introduction to the views of these three figures will be given in chapter 1.

In this book the analysis of the early stages of various religious traditions will undermine the liberal point of view. In addition, at the end of chapter 4, the chapter on early Hinduism, a critique of how John Hick would interpret early Hinduism will be given.

The major alternative to this liberal tradition has been conservatives who insist that their religious point of view is absolutely unique. Those who take this perspective are mostly Jews, Christians, or Muslims. Hindus often think that other religious traditions are very much like their own.

Whereas liberals think of religion as a genus and various religious orientations as species of that genus, conservatives deny this. Because of their belief in the uniqueness of their own religious orientation they do not consider their own religious orientation as belonging to the general category of religion. Chapter 2 will present the views of the two most influential Christian conservatives—Thomas Aquinas and Karl Barth. A critique of their points of view will also be given.

In chapter 3 an alternative outline will be given of the nature of religious views of life. According to this outline religious views of life embody beliefs or assumptions that fall into a set of categories which are referred to as the elements of religion. For example, religious views of life embody some kind of value emphasis, some view of human nature, and some view of God, the gods, Brahman, Nirvana, Dharma-Kaya, or similar kind of "things." Religious views of life involve interpretations of the elements of

# Introduction

religion that fit together into a whole. One does theology by criticizing or defending interpretations of these elements.

It is important to note two things about these interpretations. One is that truth is often applicable. For example, people will differ when it comes to understanding human nature, but few will deny that the concept of truth is applicable here. The other thing to note is that over time the interpretations of these elements often change. When an interpretation of one of the elements changes, then an interpretation of the others will also change. Interpretations fit together like a puzzle and have to adjust to one another.

The liberal regards these changes as only cultural. The arguments here will show that the changes are more than cultural, but a matter of substance.

To analyze and discuss every religious view of life would be an impossible task. We are going to take a clue that John Hick uses in addressing this problem. He discusses four major religious traditions in the hope that this would shed light on religion in some breadth. We will analyze early Hinduism, early Buddhism, biblical Judaism, and early Christianity. This will be done in chapters 4 through 9. Hopefully an analysis of these four early traditions will shed light on other religious traditions. If it doesn't, something can be seen to be accomplished when shedding light on the character of these religious traditions.

Obviously not everyone is going to be happy with this view of religion. In chapters 10 and 11 criticisms are going to be anticipated. Some Christians will reject this view of religion because of their view of Christ. They will claim that a proper understand of Christ is not compatible with the view of religion given here. A response will be given to that objection by discussing various views of Jesus, Christology. The argument will be that the appropriate kind of Christology is compatible with the view of religion presented in this book. That's the subject of chapter 10.

Some individuals will argue that the view of religion presented here is not compatible with Zen because Zen plays down the role of language in the context of religion. This book presents a way of doing theology. Theology involves theory, and attachment to theory is a basic human problem, according to Zen. A famous statement in Zen says, "A special transmission outside the Scriptures; no dependence upon words and letters." The critic will argue that no kind of theology can capture the substance of Zen. A critique of that point of view will be given. Rather than cover all of the different schools of Zen the discussion will focus on one of the influential ones, Rinzai Zen. That will be the subject of chapter 11.

If theology involves interpretations of the elements of religion, and a criticism and defense of those interpretations, it is appropriate to show how this can be done. This will be subject of chapters 12 through 15.

O. Hobart Mowrer and John Bradshaw are two therapists who integrate a religious orientation into their therapy. In the fifties Mowrer became popular for his view that the concept of sin ought to be part of the vocabulary of psychology. His view of therapy and his view of sin involved criticisms of John Calvin and Sigmund Freud. His views will be discussed in chapter 12. This chapter concludes with a critique of Advaita Vedanta, a Hindu theology, and a critique of Theravada Buddhism.

John Bradshaw was the host of a Public Broadcast System series Bradshaw On: The Family, and also a series Eight Stages of Man. He is relevant here because he uses the tools of therapy to introduce a view of religion significantly different from Mowrer. His views will be discussed in chapter 13.

Mowrer and Bradshaw both focus on the well-being of the individual person. It is another thing to address the nature of and the well-being of a society as a whole and the institutions within it. Chapters 12 and 13 are about the former; chapters 14 and 15 are about the latter.

Chapter 14 will examine the views of Walter Rauschenbusch; chapter 15 the views of Reinhold Niebuhr. In the early twentieth century the social gospel movement evolved. Rauschenbusch was a prime spokesperson for that. He was also a liberal pacifist. Reinhold Niebuhr was a very popular theologian who was critical of the pacifism of liberals. His point of view is called Christian realism.

# PART 1

What Is a Religious View of Life?

# 1

# The Liberal Perspective

THE LIBERAL VIEW OF the world religions sees the roots of religion to be in religious experience. It then goes on to claim that the same religious ultimate, God, or Being-Itself, manifests itself in all of these experiences. Their view is that differences among the various religious traditions are due to differences in culture. Cultures function like glasses that color what people see. The same religious ultimate, however, undergirds all of them.

Recently Stephen Prothero has criticized this view in his book *God Is Not One*. Unlike this book, however, he does not recommend a view of the nature of religious views of life.

We are going to look briefly at the three most influential figures in the liberal tradition: Friedrich Schleiermacher, Paul Tillich, and John Hick.

## FRIEDRICH SCHLEIERMACHER (1768-1834)

Any Christian familiar with contemporary thinking should realize that there are many critics on a number of fronts who are hostile to any kind of religious faith. They find creeds and doctrines to be repulsive. They find views of the Bible and cosmological beliefs belonging to the first century or earlier to be simplistic. Nothing about faith appears attractive to them. This was also the world that Friedrich Schleiermacher lived in the late eighteenth and early nineteenth century.

# Part 1—What Is a Religious View of Life?

Schleiermacher was raised in a devout family in tune with the orthodoxy of the day. His mother was concerned about the secular skepticism that permeated the intellectual culture of the time. She thus entered him into a Moravian school, a school run by the Brethren. That community had a significant influence on his religious life. He had religious experiences that influenced him significantly. His mind had a skeptical bent, however, that did not fit with the Moravian community.

To understand the early Schleiermacher it is important to see him in his historical context. In the late eighteenth century he was in Berlin where he participated in the development of German Romanticism. His life and friendships were closely linked to those who were shaping the movement. This included Schlegel, a literary critic who helped found the *Athenaeum*. This magazine gave the romantics a place to present and discuss their views. Schleiermacher made his contributions. Schlegel and Schleiermacher worked together on a project of translating the works of Plato. Plato ended up affecting and shaping his theology.

This work of translating led him to consider seriously the problems of understanding ancient texts. This led him to consider seriously how language functions, how it works. Later when he lectured on Scripture he discussed the problems of understanding texts and language in general. He lectured on the basis of notes. Scholars have organized his notes and published them in a book entitled *Hermeneutics: The Handwritten Manuscripts*. In those lectures he developed the theoretical background for the higher criticism which developed later in the nineteenth century. Scholars have often been critical of his discussion of hermeneutics. It is this author's view that they often have not understood it. In an article entitled "Schleiermacher's Hermeneutic and Its Critics," this author explained and defended his view of hermeneutics.

Schleiermacher was a member of a group of romantics who were critical of the rationalists who emphasized the relevance of reason to capture the nature of reality. Here Kant's *Critique of Pure Reason*, written in 1781, was of benefit to them. They also had no taste for the empiricists whose path seemed to lead to radical skepticism, as in the case of David Hume. Instead they emphasized intuitions and feelings which gave them a mystical bent.

Unlike some of the materialists in France, the romantics were not necessarily hostile to religion. They perceived, however, in the religious establishment and among the population, simple-minded stuff that repelled them. This left a door open to someone with roots in the romantic tradition to come to the defense of religion. Schleiermacher drove a huge bus through that door. The name on the bus was *On Religion: Speeches to Its Cultured Despisers*, which was written in 1799. Not all of the romantics got on the bus, but it was a game-changing type of work.

The basic thrust of this book is that the despisers of religion had rejected it because of its doctrines and dogmas, which he says are nothing but empty shells. Instead, he says, "I would show you from what human tendency religion proceeds and how it belongs to what is for you highest and dearest."[1] Wow! What they value most is embedded in religion.

What do people value the most? At the heart of the religious life he finds piety. In pious exultations of the mind one can find "immediate feeling of the Infinite and the Eternal."[2] He says,

> The contemplation of the pious is the immediate consciousness of the universal existence of all finite things, in and through the Infinite, and of all temporal things in and through the Eternal. Religion is to seek this and find it in all that lives and moves, in all growth and change, in all doing and suffering. It is to have life and know life in immediate feeling . . . an existence in the Infinite and Eternal.[3]

It is clear here that he is intoxicated with the spirit of German Romanticism and is addressing an audience that shares his orientation. That is why the book became very popular.

Why for Schleiermacher is religion a product of religious experience? It is in part because of what we are and in part because of what religion is. We are beings who by nature have feeling. At the heart of religion lies piety and piety belongs primarily to the feeling aspect of our lives. Through contemplations and exultations of the mind linked to piety, a person becomes aware of the Infinite and the Eternal, becomes aware of God. To find God is to have life and know life in immediate feeling.

Are there any similarities between the views of Schleiermacher and what is found in this book? We agree that theology ought not to be based on speculative philosophy, à la Hegel. It ought to be linked to the religious dimension of our lives. Whether feelings represent a special dimension of our lives seems to this author controversial. Religion, however, does

---

1. Schleiermacher, *On Religion*, 11–12.
2. Ibid., 16.
3. Ibid., 36.

involve feelings and passions. Interpretations of religion do involve feelings and passions. The function of theology is to critique and defend various interpretations.

## PAUL TILLICH (1886–1965)

Tillich shares a number of things in common with Schleiermacher. For one thing, both of them became very popular. Three editions of Schleiermacher's major theological work, *Christian Faith*, came out while he was still living. He was recognized by intellectuals of his time and eventually became regarded as the father of modern theology.

In the 1950s both *Time* and the *Saturday Evening Post* had articles devoted to Tillich. His special lectures in the Rockefeller Chapel at the University of Chicago were attended by throngs of students and classes on him tended to thrive.

When this author interviewed for a job after graduate school, he talked to a couple of professors who had a fondness for Tillich. I said that I had difficulties with him. Even though I had written a master's thesis on him, I never warmed up to the substance of his philosophy. Their response to my comment was, "Who else?" The implication was that there were not a lot of serious alternatives to Tillich on the contemporary philosophy of religion scene. This was during the sixties. I should have mentioned that process philosophy and process theology are serious alternatives. Charles Hartshorne and John Cobb are in this tradition. Since the sixties the philosophy of religion scene has change significantly. John Hick is probably now the most influential figure.

Like Schleiermacher, Tillich rejected speculative metaphysics and focused on religious experience. To understand Tillich's view of religious experience, one should take into consideration his understanding of the ultimate and his view of symbols. The word "God" for Tillich serves two functions. The statement "God is Being-itself" is non-symbolic. It is literally true. "God," however, functions also as a symbol. Symbols participate in the reality to which they point.

If a person names a pet "God" or "Christ," many are going to find this deeply offensive, irreligious. For Tillich this indicates that these words are symbols which participate in the divine to which they point.

A person cannot create or destroy symbols. They have a history of their own. A true symbol, Tillich says, must have an element of sacredness about it and provide power and meaning to the person who recognizes it. Ultimate power and meaning is Being-itself. Thus symbols which sustain lives and give meaning to lives participate in the Ultimate, Being-itself.

Consider the words "freedom" and "America." In the United States they are powerful symbols that give meaning and significance to life. We are all in a sense religious creatures because we all recognize symbols through which we find power and meaning. According to Tillich when we find power and meaning through symbols we participate in ultimate power and meaning, Being-itself. As a Christian theologian Tillich goes on to critique certain symbols and to defend the significance of certain Christian symbols.

There is a possible weakness in Tillich's view of symbols. According to Mackenzie Brown, Tillich believed that a nation, a sex figure, and a race can function appropriately as symbols of the ultimate as long they are not regarded as the ultimate.[4] Whether or not this is true, I'll leave it up for others to determine. The view of this author is that a person should reflect on the values embedded within symbols, and symbols should be critiqued in part by the values they imply.

Are there any similarities between the views of Tillich and what is found in this book? For Tillich symbols convey power and meaning. Later I am going to talk about "elements of religion." These are various types of beliefs and assumptions important to religious views of life. One of the elements of religion is called "spiritual hypotheticals." These are views wherein human fulfillment and happiness can best be found. If a symbol conveys power, then this symbol will be seen as a way of finding happiness and well-being. One of the other elements of religion is values, things that are important from a moral as well as a non-moral point of view. If a symbol conveys meaning, then it will be linked to values that are considered important. Thus Tillich's symbols are linked to two of the elements of religion. These elements will be explained and discussed in chapter 3.

## JOHN HICK

John Hick was born in 1922 in Yorkshire, England, and is still active as a philosopher. He has become a prolific author. His website lists him as authoring twenty-nine books. He is vice president of the British Society for the Philosophy of Religion and of the World Congress of Faiths. He gave the

---

4. Brown, *Ultimate Concern*, 11.

## Part 1 — What Is a Religious View of Life?

Gifford Lectures in 1986–1987 and won the 1996 Grawemeyer Award in religion. Recently the John Hick Centre for Philosophy of Religion opened. The center is located in the University of Birmingham's School of Philosophy, Theology, and Religion. Its role is to foster excellence in research in the area of philosophy of religion from a global perspective.

His book *Philosophy of Religion* (1963) is probably the most used book in philosophy of religion courses. In the first edition of the book, he begins with an analysis of the Judaic-Christian concept of God as that view has been developed historically in the Middle Ages, in classical theism. He then discusses the arguments for belief in such a God and the arguments against such a belief. Finally, he discusses the question of the immortality of the soul. This approach is in the tradition of Thomas Aquinas because it focuses on a particular notion of God and the arguments for and against such a being.

In the second edition of his book, dated ten years later, 1973, he shows discomfort with his first edition. This book follows the same pattern, but now besides a chapter on the immortality of the soul, he has a chapter on karma and reincarnation. This is followed by a final chapter entitled "The Conflicting Truth Claims of Different Religions." In his article "On Conflicting Truth Claims," he says, "When I meet a devout Jew, or Muslim, or Sikh, or Hindu, or Buddhist in whom the fruits of openness to the divine Reality are gloriously evident, I cannot realistically regard the Christian experience of the divine as authentic and their non-Christian experience inauthentic."[5] In other words, the root of these religious orientations lies in religious experiences, experiences of the same divine reality.

Hick recognizes the difficulty in discussing all of the various religious traditions. He thus chooses to focus on four of them: Hinduism, Buddhism, Islam, and Christianity. The relevant questions at this point are: What is the logic that holds these traditions together, and how do we account for their differences?

What they have in common, he says, is their "soteriological structure." What's that? "They offer a transition from a radically unsatisfactory state to a limitlessly better one."[6] Here's another description: "In each case, salvation/liberation consists in a new and limitlessly better quality of existence which comes about in the transition from self-centeredness to Reality-centeredness."[7]

---

5. Hick, "On Conflicting Truth Claims," 488.
6. Hick, "On Grading Religions," 452.
7. Ibid., 453.

## The Liberal Perspective

There are two things that "better quality of existence" can refer to. It can mean helping achieve what the ideal individual or society is like. Clearly that is often important to religious views of life. It can also mean achieving happiness and well-being for the individual person or the society. That is also often important to religious views of life. In one case it is a belief about values, and in the other case a belief about what I call "spiritual hypotheticals." These are views of wherein lies the happiness and well-being of the individual or the society. There are also negative spiritual hypotheticals. These are views wherein lies the destruction, the deterioration, the spiritual death of the individual person or society.

Hick calls the test for a better quality of existence pragmatic. This would suggest that if a person finds a particular religious orientation useful, helpful, then it has validity. That would seem to indicate that the notion of truth is not applicable here. What would follow is that there is no truth as to wherein human happiness can best be found. This book will argue that they can contain truth. It will also show how spiritual hypotheticals are found in four religious traditions. In the last chapters' various spiritual hypotheticals will be assessed—chapters 12, 13, 14, and 15.

For Hick, if a concern about a better quality of existence is what religious orientations have in common, what accounts for their differences? As mentioned above—it is the cultural, historical context in which they are found. People perceive the Ultimate through colored glasses. The color is determined by cultural contexts. The differences between Brahman, Nirvana, Dharma Kaya, Yahweh, God, and Allah are cultural.

What does this book have in common with the views of John Hick? In teaching courses on philosophy of religion this author found it frustrating that the books in philosophy of religion were usually not about religion. Books in philosophy of science are about science, and books about philosophy of law are about law. Books about philosophy of religion, however, usually focus on classical theism, much like the first edition of Hick's *Philosophy of Religion*. It is thus important that he came to recognize the reality of religious pluralism and take it seriously.

This book also makes use of his view of the soteriological structure of religion. It draws a distinction, however, between the value dimension of soteriology and what might be called the happiness dimension involving spiritual hypotheticals.

# Part 1 — What Is a Religious View of Life?

## SUMMARY

We have seen that these theological giants see religion as rooted in experiences of the religious ultimate. Schleiermacher appealed to the experiences of his audience: experiences of highs where their minds were exalted; experiences in nature that moved them and where they felt life. This is the realm of religion—not the doctrines that are dry, empty husks.

Tillich appealed to experiences that give meaning to life and gave power to sustain life. These were powerful symbols that shaped life. For a Christian these were often the cross and the figure of Jesus. For early Hindus it was often the figure of Indra that turned them on. For early Buddhists it was the portrait of Gautama the Buddha and stories about him. The difference between the religious and the non-religious is not the recognition and non-recognition of symbols, but the nature of the symbols. Through these symbols power and meaning are found; Being-Itself is found.

Hick focuses on the redemptive power of religion. It changes and transforms life. Through religion people find salvation, liberation; they find life at its very best. Instead of life being self-centered, life becomes focused on the Ultimate.

For Hick the difference between Brahman and Yahweh is cultural. To use the language of Kant, we can say that Brahman and Yahweh are phenomenal realities. Beyond them is noumenal reality, the Ultimate.

The view of religion in this book makes use of Hick's emphasis on the redemptive character of religion. It draws a distinction, however, between value dimension of redemption and the happiness or well-being dimension of redemption.

At the end of the chapter on Hinduism, a critique will be given of John Hick's interpretation of early Hinduism.

The view of religion presented in this book shares something common with all of these theologians. However, the role that metaphysics plays in the philosophies of Thomas Aquinas and Hegel is rejected. The view of religion presented here differs in taking seriously the differences among religious views of life. It takes seriously the differences between the Brahman of the Upanishads and the God of the prophet Amos; between Theravada Buddhism and Mahayana Buddhism; and between Paul and the Synoptic Gospels. It is denied that these differences are cultural.

# 2

# The Conservative Perspective

WE LIVE IN A world with a vast array of religious traditions—Hinduism, Buddhism, Taoism, Sikhs, Judaism, Muslims, Christian and many others. Individuals in these traditions think that they have an understanding of what is truly important, true, and real, but they differ radically. Those conflicting understandings can't equally capture the truth. We thus have a problem. The liberals, in the tradition of Schleiermacher, Hick and Tillich, say that there is no real problem here. The differences are really cultural. Behind the differences there exists the same religious ultimate. The conservative—Christian, Muslim, or Jew—accepts that there are real differences, but denies that his or her own faith should be put in the same category as other religious traditions. It is absolutely unique and special because of the way God has revealed himself in it. To take seriously the study of other religious traditions is to confuse what is human with what is divine. God is known as he reveals himself. Conservatives differ on how this revelation is to be understood. Many Christians have identified with Thomas Aquinas (1225–1274). More recently many have been attracted to Karl Barth (1886–1968). These kinds of religious conservatism are also present in Islam and Judaism.[1] We are going to limit our discussion to manifestations of it in the Christian tradition.

---

1. 8 Hindus often think of Judaism, Christianity, and Islam as variations of their own religious tradition.

Part 1—What Is a Religious View of Life?

## THOMAS AQUINAS (1225-1274)

In the Roman Catholic tradition Aquinas is considered the church's greatest theologian and philosopher. Pope Benedict XV declared his teaching to be their own. Luther and Calvin both rejected his theology, but eventually many conservative Protestants came to identify with him.[2]

Aquinas defends the uniqueness of Christian faith in his *Summa Theologica* where he discusses the nature of sacred doctrine. He begins by asking the question of whether we need a science besides the philosophical sciences. Here he is reflecting the influence of Aristotle who considered all knowledge to be found in some kind of philosophical science. Do we need a science besides the philosophical sciences? Aquinas answers his question by appealing to the inspiration of Scripture and by quoting one of Paul's letters, 2 Timothy 3:16: "All scripture is inspired by God profitable for teaching, for reprove, for correction, to and for training in righteousness."[3] He then states the reason for this inspiration. He says, "It was necessary for the salvation of man that certain truths which exceed human reason should be known by revelation."[4]

What is being said here, in effect, is that a study of nature and normal kinds of reasoning does not give us the truths which are necessary for salvation. We thus need revelation. Why should we consider that there is such a thing as salvation? If there is, why is it that the Christian Bible gives it to us? Why not the Koran or the Vedas? Those questions do not arise. Conveniently, however, Paul purportedly tells us that the Christian Bible gives us this information. The science of sacred doctrine is thus rooted in Scripture and in revelation.

Theology is to be rooted Scripture and revelation, but is it a science? He refers to an adversary as saying that sacred doctrine cannot be a science because it proceeds from faith. The reply is that there are two kinds of sciences. Some are based on the natural light of reason, but others are derived from a higher science. Sacred doctrine, he says, belongs to the latter because it proceeds from "the science of God and the blessed."[5] To explain this, he says that the science of God and the blessed is divine knowledge. In

---

2. See Rogers and McKim, *Authority and Interpretation*, chap. 3.
3. Biblical references throughout are to the RSV.
4. Aquinas, *Basic Writings*, 6.
5. Ibid.

## The Conservative Perspective

other words, sacred doctrine is rooted in Scripture, revelation, and involves divine knowledge.

Aquinas then goes on to say that sacred doctrine is nobler than other sciences because of the dignity of its subject matter, but also because of its certitude. Whereas human reason is capable of error, divine knowledge, he says, cannot err. Sacred doctrine is thus rooted in Scripture and revelation. It has a firm foundation that is absolutely certain because it is a product of divine knowledge which cannot err.

This is the classic statement of the doctrine of the inerrancy of Scripture. He goes on to say that this science is both speculative and practical. It is more speculative because it is concerned more with divine things as opposed to human actions.

Reading through this section of the *Summa* can take a person's breath away. Wow! Do you mean that if someone quotes a passage of Scripture there is divine knowledge here that is absolutely certain that came directly from God? A sophisticated Thomist will find places in the writings of Aquinas to justify a toning down of what is said here, but his intention here is clear. He considers theology to be a science founded in Scripture that is absolutely certain.

Note should be taken that this view has run into a number of road blocks. First, what is it that is supposed to be inerrant? Apparently what the various authors of the Bible wrote—authors such as Paul and the authors of the various gospels. A problem lies in the fact that we do not have what Paul wrote or what any of the other authors of the biblical books wrote. Here Bart Ehrman's *Misquoting Jesus* is a valuable source. He is a textual critic who has studied the history of how we got the various versions of the New Testament.

Before there was a printing press copies of all manuscripts were hand copied, word for word. Sometimes unintended mistakes were made; sometimes a copyist would change what he thought was a mistake in what he read. Sometimes theology and ideology played a role. The earliest copy we have of Paul's Letter to the Galatians is dated 200 CE.[6] That is one hundred and fifty years after Paul would have written it. Since there were many churches in Galatia, we do not know how many copies he would have had someone write. If there were many copies were the copies exactly the same? Did he dictate word for word?

---

6. Ehrman, *Misquoting Jesus*, 60.

## Part 1—What Is a Religious View of Life?

We also know that writing takes place in historical contexts. Understanding Scripture requires understanding the language, the culture and the historical context out of which it arose. We will see an example of this in chapter 9 in a discussion of the Synoptic Gospels. In this area there is no absolute certainty. This kind of thing was of no concern to Aquinas.

In the latter part of the twentieth century there were several prominent conservatives who had accepted the doctrine of inerrancy, but who gave it up and published books to justify their positions. This included *The Divine Inspiration of Scripture*, by William Abraham; *The Authority and Interpretation of Scripture: A Historical Approach*, by Jack Rogers and Donald McKim; and *The Debate about the Bible: Inerrancy versus Infallibility*, by Steven Davis.

There are several points upon which they agreed. First, they agreed that the view of inerrancy is not derived from Scripture but imported from the outside. Aquinas quotes 2 Timothy 3:16. What was the Bible of the early Christians? It was the Jewish Bible. Jesus was killed about 30 CE. The earliest New Testament writings come from Paul who was writing in the fifties. The latest writings were in the first couple of decades of the second century. The first list of books to be candidates for the New Testament was written in the last part of the second century. No agreement on the list was reached until the last part of the fourth century. Second Timothy 3:16 did not refer to that set of books.

The prophets made statements of the form, "Thus says the Lord!" The same cannot be said of either the Jewish or the Christian Bible taken as a whole. We do not find statements of the form, "Thus says the Lord, 'so and so begat so and so, who begat so and so, who begat so and so.'" At the beginning of the Gospel of Luke the author says that many have written about the figure of Jesus, and thus it seemed good for him to do the same (Luke 1:4). No reference to having had a revelation.

Note also that 2 Timothy 3:16 makes use of the word "inspiration." The view of Thomas, however, was that Scripture is a matter of revelation. There can be inspiration without revelation, and inspiration does not require inerrancy. This is the basic point of William Abraham's book, *The Divine Inspiration of Scripture*.

Does revelation require inerrancy? This is at least controversial. In the latter part of this chapter we will examine the views of Karl Barth. He emphasizes revelation, but rejects the doctrine of inerrancy.

Usually when a few theologians make a shift in their theology, it is not a big deal. However, in reaction to the detractors who gave up on the doctrine of inerrancy, a convention was convened in Chicago in 1979. It was called the International Conference on Biblical Inerrancy. From this conference came a series of papers which make up the collection of writings found in a book entitled *Inerrancy*, edited by Norman Geisler. The book has a list of articles which state what the leaders of this conference believe. Article 12 says, "We further deny that scientific hypotheses about earth history may properly be used to overturn the teachings of Scripture on creation and the flood."[7] The thrust of this is to say that Scripture is a statement of divine knowledge which cannot be undermined by the methods of science.

We thus have a doctrine not derived from Scripture, but imported from the outside. It claims the inerrancy of something we do not have—the original manuscripts. It is a doctrine which has no justification. In addition, it leads to rejecting what modern science has to say about the earth and its age because Scripture is regarded as containing divine knowledge which is absolutely certain.

## KARL BARTH (1886–1968)

Karl Barth is like Aquinas in his emphasis on the uniqueness of Christian faith, a uniqueness linked to revelation. He has a different view of revelation, however.

Aquinas begins his discussion of theology in *Summa Theologica* by arguing that sacred doctrine is a science. For Barth there is no argument here. He begins his discussion by just noting that theology is considered a science, a science of God. He notes that many things can be noted by that word and there are many kinds of theology.

For Barth the kinds of gods and the kinds of theology seem infinite. He says, "There is no man who does not have his own god or gods as the object of his highest desire and trust, or as the basis of his deepest loyalty and commitment. There is no one who is not to this extent a theologian."[8] In other words, theology is inevitable. There is no philosophy or any worldview that does not have some such divinity, one which is an object of highest desire and trust; one that involves one's deepest loyalty and commitment.

---

7. Geisler, *Inerrancy*, 496.
8. Barth, *Evangelical Theology*, 3.

## Part 1—What Is a Religious View of Life?

Every philosophy is a kind of theology. The object of such a theology may be nature, or it may be reason, or a "redeeming nothingness into which man would be destined to disappear."[9]

This is analogous to Tillich's view that everyone recognizes symbols through which they find power and meaning. Everyone is then, in a sense, religious.

The background of this book is the philosophy of Wittgenstein and what is sometimes called Ordinary Language Philosophy. The latter involve individuals such as John Austin, Gilbert Ryle, and Peter Strawson. Philosophers in these traditions seek to understand how language functions in general, and how it functions in the context of logic, science, ethics, law, and religion. On the first point, it is interesting to note that Schleiermacher was concerned about this problem. His views are worked out in his lectures on hermeneutics. If one is going to interpret Scripture, he believed, one then needs to know how language functions in general and then apply it to Scripture. As mentioned earlier, my article "Schleiermacher's Hermeneutic and Its Critics" is based on linking Schleiermacher's hermeneutics to contemporary philosophy of language. It defends his point of view. It is hard to see how a concern about how language functions involves a god. If Scripture is important, then understanding how to interpret it is important.

The second point involves the investigation on how language functions in the context of logic, science, ethics, law, and religion. They do that to help understand these areas. This book seeks to carry out that project in the context of religion. If seeking to understand these things is a god, then such a god is important.

Barth says that his interest is in evangelical theology. He wants to mark it off, not to imply any kind evaluation of theologies in general, but to clarify the uniqueness of evangelical theology. Theologies, he says, shed light on the gods they represent. Each theology, therefore, presents itself as the best. He does not wish to play that game, however. Evangelical theology ought not to present itself as embodying divine wisdom because it is devoted to God. He says, "For the very reason that it is devoted to the God who proclaims himself in the Gospel, evangelical theology cannot claim for itself that authority which belongs to him alone."[10] This seems to be directed to Aquinas who says that theology contains propositions based on divine knowledge. The argument is that since evangelical theology is de-

9. Ibid., 4.
10. Ibid., 6.

voted to God who embodies the supreme authority, it cannot claim divine knowledge.

What can be said about this God? Two things: he transcends our minds and he discloses himself. Barth says, "He transcends not only the undertakings of all other men but also the enterprise of evangelical theologians."[11] This is analogous to Kant's noumenal reality—ultimate reality which we cannot know. This differs from phenomenal reality, which is reality we can know. This is also analogous to Nirvana in Buddhism. In early Buddhism the words that apply to this world do not apply to Nirvana. It is too transcendent.

Barth also says, "He is the God who again and again discloses himself anew and must be discovered anew, the God over whom theology neither has nor receives sovereignty."[12] This disclosure is, of course, revelation; God revealing himself.

If God transcends our minds, however, how are we to be able to recognize any revelation of it? Would not any revelation of it go beyond our ability to understand? Maybe "it" would be the appropriate way to refer the ultimate.

For Barth to talk of revelation requires talk of Christ because Christ, he says, is the revelation of God. He says, "When we say, I believe in God, the concrete meaning is that I believe in the Lord Jesus Christ."[13] This theology is sometimes called a Christ-centered theology.

Even though Barth refers to Scripture as having binding force, it is not considered inerrant. It is, however, referred to as the "Word of God." What does that mean? Scripture witnesses to Jesus, to the Christ. Referring to the phrase "Word of God" he says, "We mean by it that Holy Scripture as the witness of the prophets and the apostles to this one Word of God, to Jesus, the man out of Israel who is God's Christ, our Lord and King in eternity."[14]

Scripture is thus not divine knowledge, as it was for Thomas, but a witness to Jesus, the Word that became flesh. One meaning of the word "Word" (*Logos*) is reason, and in Platonism this Logos is regarded as timeless. Barth, however, understands the Word in terms of revelation and uses the phrase "living Word of God." This revelation is a product of God's sovereign decision and should not be evaluated in terms of rational reflection.

11. Ibid.
12. Ibid.
13. Barth, *Dogmatics in Outline*, 17.
14. Ibid.

## PART 1—WHAT IS A RELIGIOUS VIEW OF LIFE?

This would rob God of his transcendence. Barth's Christology will be discussed in a later chapter when we discuss various types of Christology.

What about Barth's claim about the extreme transcendence of God? He says that God transcends the enterprise of all men, including the enterprise of evangelical theologians. Why should anyone believe that? There are two ways of considering this. If one were to give reasons for God's transcendence, then Barth would say that this would rob God of his transcendence. Theologies give reasons for their gods. For Barth that indicates that their gods aren't truly transcendent. There is something above them—these reasons. One can see here why Barth's theology is considered as being a form of fideism based on faith and faith alone. For him to give reasons for a belief in a particular kind of God is to run afoul of robbing that God of transcendence.

If Christ has a special link to revelation and no reason can be given to make this link, then the door is open to make all kinds of linkage. Why not Marilyn Monroe as a link to the supreme goddess? In the traditional Roman Empire, that kind of linkage was made to the emperor, Caesar Augustus; to whom the title Divi Filius (son of the divine) was added.

## SUMMARY

Thomas regarded arguments for the existence of God as sound. Barth doesn't. That difference is not as important as it may seem. For Thomas, the entire understanding of salvation is based on an appeal to revelation. Thus for both, revelation is primary. Their significant difference lies in their understanding of the nature of revelation.

To understand an author one needs to understand the historical context in which he or she wrote. It is important to note that Thomas wrote before the Renaissance and the rise of modern science. He could command the respect of the intellectuals of his day because of his philosophy. There were no problems arising because of science.

He lived in a Christian culture where he addressed Christians. Other religious traditions and other scriptures did not seem to concern him. When he said, in effect, we need revelation, no one said to him, "Why not the Koran or the Vedas?"

The differences between Thomas and Barth lie primarily on their understanding of revelation. Barth knows modern science. He doesn't want to reject it. Therefore, the inerrancy of Scripture is rejected. In both cases the

## The Conservative Perspective

appeal to revelation is really based on faith. For Thomas, it was his faith in Scripture that led him to quote it and try to use it to justify his view of theology. In addition, of course, the Scripture he was referring to, 2 Timothy 3:16, was not the Christian Scriptures. The early Christians had only the Jewish Bible.

The one thing that Barth added as a support to his perspective is his views that everyone has a god. If everyone has a god, then we ought not to criticize him for having one also. That move, however, opens the door to all kinds of gods and goddesses. From the perspective of this book, it can be said that a commitment to understand the nature of religious views of life can hardly qualify as a god. Besides, if Scripture is important, then a commitment to understand language and how to interpret Scripture is equally important.

Barth considers himself as accepting modern science, but he really does not take seriously what biblical scholars have said about Scriptures. For example, he does not address Albert Schweitzer's view of the historical Jesus.

# 3

# A Wittgensteinian Perspective

WHAT IS A RELIGIOUS view of life? A basic concern of this book is to address that question. All kinds of philosophers have written about the nature of religion. The concern here is with a particular discussion that has gone on in the linguistic philosophical tradition. Sometimes this kind of philosophy is identified by its links to the Universities of Oxford and Cambridge, but it is misleading to limit it this way. Two of the earliest collections of essays in this tradition are *Logic and Language*, first series, 1951, and second series, 1953. This led to two collections of essays relating to religion: *New Essays in Philosophical Theology* and *Metaphysical Beliefs: Three Essays*. Behind the work of many of these philosophers lies the work of the later Wittgenstein. His *Blue and Brown Books* (1958) were notes dictated in English to Cambridge students in 1933–1934. His most important work, *Philosophical Investigations*, was published posthumously in 1953. He died of cancer in 1951. *On Certainty* was a book published in 1969 that is based on notes he wrote just before his death.

The phrase "later Wittgenstein" is used here because the direction of his thinking changed course. His earlier point of view is found in *Tractatus Logico-Philosophicus*, published in 1921. The focus of his thinking in his later works is to seek to understand how language functions, on how it is used. The phrase "ordinary language philosophy" is sometimes used here. "Ordinary" does not mean a common use, but rather a standard use. The use of the language of science may not be common, but in science words have a standard use understood by the scientific community. His philosophy has led to a study of how language is used in logic, mathematics, science, ethics, law, and, of course, religion.

This book is not going to trace the large variety of things philosophers in this tradition have said about religion. A survey of them can be found in William Blackstone's book *The Problem of Religious Knowledge*. Instead, a model for understanding religious views of life is going to be presented and then defended by looking at a number of religious traditions. Before doing that, however, we are going to discuss a particular way of looking at religion that can be very appealing to a philosopher influenced by Wittgenstein.

## IS A RELIGIOUS VIEW OF LIFE A LANGUAGE GAME?

In the search to understand how language functions, Wittgenstein introduced the concept of language game. When we have a community of people who agree on how to use a set of words and how to use them, then Wittgenstein says that we have a language game. The larger point here is that language is a community affair where people learn how to use it and agree as to how it is to be used. One of Wittgenstein's dictums is, "Don't ask what a word means; ask how it is used." Some philosophers see here a way to shed light on the nature of religious language. Religious language is taught in a community, and there are rules for its proper use. It would thus appear that a religious orientation is a community thing involving a language game. Truth is then considered as something internal to the game. People in this tradition sometimes think entirely of Christian faith, but the view implies that each religious orientation would have its own game and its own set of "truths." Each religious orientation would be a separate kind of world because rules for the use and meaning of words would always be internal to some kind of religious community and religious orientation.

William Blackstone, in effect, puts the views of R. M. Hare, J. J. C. Smart, Thomas McPherson, R. F. Holland, R. B. Braithwaite, Ronald Hepburn, and Alasdair MacIntyre in this category.[1] These individuals do not usually use the word "game." They consider, however, their religious understanding of life, or a religious understanding of life, as having an internal structure not tied logically to anything external—such as a game.

---

1. Blackstone, *Religious Knowledge*, 73–107.

## Part 1—What Is a Religious View of Life?

George Lindbeck is also in this tradition. He likens a religion to a language and a culture. He also refers to Wittgenstein as someone who has influenced him and builds on his notion of language game.[2]

For those who take a religious orientation to be a type of game, there is a problem in comparing two religious orientations because the meaning of terms in each would be internal to that religious orientation. The phrase "proper move" means one thing in checkers, another thing in chess. Its meaning is determined by the rules of the game. The meanings of king, queen, and knight are determined by the rules of chess. If the concept of language game applied to each religious orientation, then there would be no way to explain the meanings of words in a particular religious orientation by the use of words outside of that religious orientation. From this point of view, concepts such as truth and validity would be applicable only in the context of a particular religious orientation. Someone who has been influenced by Karl Barth might find this view attractive. The language of faith is a game all of its own and is rooted in faith alone.

A problem arises when one applies the concept of language game to a religious orientation. No matter how you specify the community of a particular religious orientation, one will find different points of view in that community—some disagreement on the rules. On the other hand, one will also find people outside of that orientation who will have similar views. Start by identifying a religious orientation as the religious beliefs and practices of a particular congregation. Any congregation, however, will involve people who have some differences with respect to their understanding of Christian faith. Besides, other congregations are clearly going to have much in common with this congregation. If we identify a particular orientation with a denomination, the problem multiplies. There will be more differences within and many similarities outside the denomination.

Religious traditions change over time. The concept of game cannot help us to understand these changes. One can say that a particular religious orientation changes here, and here, and here, but there would be no way one can understand the nature of these changes. A goal of the analysis of religion presented here is to enable us to understand these changes.

---

2. Lindbeck, *Nature of Doctrine*, 33.

A Wittgensteinian Perspective

## WHAT ARE RELIGIOUS VIEWS OF LIFE?

This chapter started by asking what a religious view of life is. First, the suggestion is that everyone has some kind of view of life. What does that mean? Everyone has a set of beliefs, assumptions, attitudes, dispositions, and feelings that significantly affect and shape his or her life. What kinds of things do we think are important? How do we spend our time, our money? What attitudes and feelings do we have toward nature, physical well-being, moral principles, the family, government, education, religious institutions? What views do we take about sex, marriage, gays, abortion? We all have beliefs, assumptions, attitudes, dispositions and feelings that significantly shape our lives.

If we can agree on that, then the next question is "What constitutes a religious view of life?" Given the multiplicity of religious views of life, it would be too much to examine every one of them. John Hick addresses this problem by focusing on four major religious traditions: Christianity, Islam, Hinduism and Buddhism. This approach leaves out primitive, or primal, religious life; the ancient religions of Asia, the Mediterranean world, and much of the religious life of China. He says, however, that this makes the task more manageable. This author is going to modify Hick's approach and focus on early Hinduism, Buddhism, biblical Judaism and early Christianity. In this kind of context Wittgenstein sometimes used the phrase "paradigm case." Paradigm cases are significant examples that shed led on a broad ranges of cases.

People who are not blind can learn to distinguish between yellow, orange, and red, but there is no clear line that distinguishes yellow from orange or orange from red. There are what Wittgenstein called borderline cases. In other words, there could be cases where it is difficult to determine whether something is Christian or pagan, or whether something is Hindu or Buddhist, it does not follow that in general we can't make these distinctions. The same can be said about the distinction between a religious view of life and something that is not a religious view of life.

If Confucianism and Taoism differ significantly from the point of view presented here, that would be interesting. It would not alter, however, the validity of what is said here. It could still be the case that significant light has been shed on early Hinduism, early Buddhism, biblical Judaism, and early Christianity.

Sometimes the question arises as to what is the Hindu's view of life. I don't think that there is something that can be called *the* Hindu's view of life or *the* Christian's view of life. What we have are many different views of life that individuals have in these four religious traditions.

## THE ELEMENTS OF RELIGION

What is the nature of religious views of life? What we want to know are the important beliefs and assumptions that shape religious orientations. The belief here is that they fall into six categories. The categories will be referred to as the elements of religion. They involve beliefs and assumptions about: (1) values, (2) happiness, (3) human nature, (4) rituals, (5) authority, and (6) God, the gods, Nirvana, Brahman, the Buddha-Body, Allah, and "things" of this type. These categories of beliefs and assumptions will be broken into various parts. It will then be shown how they are present in the early stages of four religious traditions. Let's first be clear what the categories refer to.

Values are people's beliefs and attitudes about things they consider important. The class of things that people value is open, but it includes beliefs and attitudes about nature, the material world, music, art, and food. These are non-moral values. There are also beliefs and attitudes about what is morally right, wrong, good and bad. Included here are beliefs about what the ideal person and the ideal society is like.

By happiness is meant views of wherein lies the happiness and well-being of the individual person as well as society. It also refers to views wherein the spiritual deaths of individuals or societies lie. They take the form of "if . . . then" statements. If you do such and such, then you will find happiness and well-being. These statements are called spiritual hypotheticals. This is not to suggest an otherworldly emphasis.

The spiritual hypotheticals that interest us are not about how to find one's physical well-being or happiness in marriage, but rather those that link to some kind of religious ultimate such as Nirvana or God. The Noble Eightfold Path in Buddhism is a means to expunge sorrow and suffering and to find peace and bliss. According to the first psalm the person who delights in the law of the Lord and meditates on it is like a tree that flourishes. Such a person, it says, prospers in all he does. John's gospel portrays Jesus as saying that he has come that people may have life and have it abundantly (John 10:10).

According to John Hick each of these four religious orientations has a soteriological structure. What does this mean? "They . . . offer a transition from a radically unsatisfactory state to a limitlessly better one,"[3] and "in each case, salvation/liberation consists in a new and limitlessly better quality of existence which comes about in the transition from self-centeredness to Reality-centeredness."[4]

The question to be put to John Hick is this: What is meant by a better quality of existence? What is meant by a limitlessly better state? As mentioned earlier, these phrases can refer to two different kinds of thing. They can mean helping achieve what the ideal individual or ideal society is like. It can also mean achieving happiness and well-being for the individual person or the society. In one case it is a belief about values, and in the other case a belief about spiritual hypotheticals-—views of wherein lies the happiness and well-being of the individual or the society.

In latter chapters it will be shown that spiritual hypotheticals are found in our four religious traditions. In the last four chapters various spiritual hypotheticals will be assessed—chapters 12, 13, 14, and 15.

The distinction between finding happiness and embodying the most important values is an important distinction. There have been a number of studies in which people in different cities were asked the extent to which they find happiness. The cities are then ranked on the basis of this happiness index. New York City does not usually come close to the top. Recently one of those studies looked into the question of why the residents of New York City do not fare better. It discovered that the awareness of suffering and the problems in the world adversely affected their happiness index. Interesting! It thus might end up that the value index of those living in New York City is higher than those found in some of the other cities, but their happiness index is lower. We have two indexes, a happiness index and a value index. They should not be confused. Once we examine the character of early Hinduism, a critique of John Hick will be given.

Wherever we find spiritual hypotheticals we find assumptions about human nature. We cannot have one without the other. The issue here is about what can and what cannot be achieved by human effort. In politics liberals tend to be more optimistic about what government can achieve; conservatives tend to be pessimistic. If a religious view of life emphasizes the importance of a set of laws for our well-being, then it assumes that human nature is such that those laws can be followed. If the view is that human nature is such that those laws can't be followed, that they have a

---

3. Hick, "On Grading Religions," 452.
4. Ibid., 453.

negative effect on human well-being, then those laws are not going to be emphasized. The Apostle Paul is known for his pessimistic view of human nature.

The phrase "human nature" also refers to the kind of beings we are. There are three standard views. Idealism says that we are mental or spiritual things. What is referred to as physical is really a manifestation of mind or spirit. Materialism says that the abilities humans have are dependent upon a body and what is physical. Dualism says that we are mind and body, or soul and body. These are different kinds of things. Beliefs and assumptions about human nature are the third element of religion. They include both types of view of human nature.

Beliefs and assumptions about rituals belong to the fourth element of religion. One can have a religious view of life without any recognition of rituals. They are thus not necessary to a religious view of life, but nevertheless they sometimes are important. Rituals can be regarded as something important to human well-being, but they also can function as a kind of magic to manipulate the universe. It is important to recognize the distinction.

When rituals are important then usually priests are important. Sometimes religion is centered on the priests and their rituals. Sometime they become more important than the gods.

The fifth category of belief refers to various beliefs about the proper understanding of authority. When a religious tradition develops, usually some understanding of authority will develop. Sometimes this takes time. Mention was made earlier that it was not until the last part of the fourth century CE that agreement among Christians was reached as to the contents of the New Testament.

There are two ways of considering authority. One is to begin with authority and make deductions. This is what Thomas Aquinas does with respect to Scripture. It can be called the deductive view. The other view is to give reasons and arguments to support that something is worthy of having authority. This is the inductive view.

The sixth category refers to beliefs and assumptions about God, the gods, Nirvana, Allah, and the Buddha-Body and "things" of this type. The category remains open. Nirvana is not a thing, but belongs in the sixth category. Differences exist not only between different religious traditions, but also in the same religious tradition.

The six categories are not equally important. The religious ultimate is usually seen as the embodiment of the most important values; thus the importance of the first element. The religious ultimate is sometimes seen as the source of life and well-being; thus the importance of the second element. Interpretations of the second element also assume an interpretation of the third element. The first three elements are thus significantly important.

No one can properly understand the history of the Christian understandings of life without taking into consideration the creeds, the Catholic bishops, the pope, the Bible—all of which involve some view of authority. Clearly the Torah is important to the Jewish tradition and the Vedas to the Hindu tradition. Interpretation of element five thus plays a significant role and function.

Note that assumptions and beliefs with respect to the first three elements are assumptions and beliefs that everyone has. As we grow up we learn through experience about values. When young, the emphasis is on not doing things that are dangerous; and on not eating certain things or playing with certain things that are harmful to us. As we get older the emphasis is more on doing things that are good for us. When we interact with others we learn about moral issues and moral problems, and form beliefs about the types of things are morally proper and improper. As we mature and reflect on our experiences, we form beliefs about the best ways to find happiness and well-being for ourselves and society—spiritual hypotheticals. Conclusions we reach will reflect some understanding of human nature. Note that everyone has these types of beliefs and assumptions. Thus they are referred to as the "elements of life."

## THE QUESTION OF TRUTH

Earlier it was said that the concepts of truth and validity apply to some aspects of religious views of life. Consider non-moral values. The federal Food and Drug Administration is based on the assumption that there are facts about the kinds of food and drugs that are good for us and harmful to us. Does anyone deny that there are pesticides that are harmful to us? The practice of medicine is based on the assumption that there are drugs and practices that are helpful and harmful to us. On the contemporary scene this kind of discussion is expanded to include what is good and harmful for the environment and our ecosystem.

What about views of human nature? In recent times there have been discussions of the mind-body, or soul-body, relationship. There are different points of view, but no one seems to deny that this is a factual issue.

Science has taught us much about the brain and the relationship between brain function and our abilities to function. In linguistic philosophy Gilbert Ryle's *Concept of Mind* has been very influential.

The other aspect of human nature is the question of the extent to which human beings are capable of affecting and bringing about change. The more optimistic emphasize that we can bring about changes in the future, and argue that we should bring about various changes. The more pessimistic emphasize our inability to do anything to alter what will happen in the future. The issues here seem to be empirical, ones to which notions of truth and validity are applicable. The American Constitution came out of a liberal tradition, but conservatives had a significant influence in shaping it. That's how we got the concept of checks and balances within government. Different views about this kind of thing will be discussed in our last chapters.

What is probably most controversial among the elements of life is the issue of whether moral beliefs can have validity. This is in the realm of ethical theory. It is beyond the function of this book to defend An ethical theory. For that, one should have a course or read a book on ethical theory. In this context competing ethical theories can be discussed and evaluated.

The suggestion here is that a reading of Lawrence Kohlberg's paper "Stages of Moral Development as a Basis of Moral Education" is valuable. As a cognitive psychologist he sought to give an analysis of the stages of moral development that is applicable across cultural lines. He does an empirical study of moral development in various cultures. In this analysis, the level of moral development is determined by the kinds of reasons a child will give for moral behavior. Starting with considering right to be what avoids punishment, he seeks to show that there are levels of development in a child's moral maturation. These levels, he seeks to show, are not determined by culture.

Irrespective of a person's attitude toward Kohlberg, it should be noted that we all make moral judgments. It is also the case that we should be thoughtful and reflective about the kinds of moral judgments we make. This involves being aware of different moral points of view. This is what ethical theory is all about.

## THE QUESTION OF GOD AND THE GODS

If in a particular context Yahweh is understood to embody a certain set of values, then there can be reasons not to believe in that view of Yahweh. One may find reasons to reject those values. The same is true of spiritual hypotheticals. If in a particular context Yahweh is seen as the source of happiness and well-being, involving a spiritual hypothetical, then there could be reasons not to believe in that view of Yahweh. One could find good reasons to criticize that spiritual hypothetical.

From this point of view there will always be serious questions about metaphysical systems that are independent of any religious view of life. In a religious view of life, a type six entity is intimately linked to the other elements of religion. A religious ultimate in a metaphysical system that is independent of a religious view of life will not have that linkage and those ties.

In other words, type six "entities" are understood and evaluated by reference to interpretations of the other elements. Think of a religious view of life as like a puzzle involving six pieces. The size and shape of each type of the pieces is a matter of controversy. People will argue and debate issues relating to values, spiritual hypotheticals, views of human nature, rituals, and authority. They will give arguments based on experience and reflections on experience. In this puzzle the size and shape of element six is determined by the size and shape of the other pieces. When changes occur in the first five elements, then changes occur in the understanding of God, the gods and Nirvana. We will see how this took place in early Hinduism, Buddhism, Judaism, and Christianity.

People sometimes claim that they have had religious experiences that are self-validating. The view is that the nature of a religious experience tells them what it is they have experienced. A problem exists because people with different religious orientations have what they claim as self-validating experiences. The view here is that claims to such self-validating experiences should be rejected in favor of a view that can make sense of different religious orientations.

The next step is to look at religious views of life found in early Hinduism, Buddhism, biblical Judaism, and early Christianity. The exercise is to see how interpretations of the elements of religion help us understand these religious traditions; and help us understand the changes that have taken place in them.

# Part 1 — What Is a Religious View of Life?

## SUMMARY

One person looked briefly at this view of religion and said that it reduced religion to morality. Another person did the same thing and said that this view makes Christian faith a form of Buddhism. One focused on values and the other on spiritual hypotheticals. Neither, of course, is true.

First a word about values: Note that values include non-moral as well as moral values. As the Christian tradition developed, it was the appropriate attitude toward non-moral values that became important. These dissenters from tradition were Marcion and the gnostics.

It was a surprise to learn that someone thought that this approach would reduce the Christian faith to a form of Buddhism. The person was a Catholic nun. She may have been reacting to the fact that this approach to religion does not begin with a metaphysical system as is found in Thomas Aquinas or Augustine. She may have been aware that Buddhism does not begin with any kind of metaphysical system. This approach to religion is in that tradition.

The response to that criticism is that this view of religion does not rule out the use of a metaphysical system. It merely says that it is not necessary. Any metaphysical system considered relevant in the context of religion would involve interpretations of the elements of life and ought to be critiqued on the basis of those interpretations. When we examine Hinduism, we will find in the Upanishads a metaphysical system. Criticism that will be made of it will not be because it has a metaphysical system. Any criticisms will be based on its interpretation of values, spiritual hypotheticals and views of human nature. We will not rely on a principle of authority.

The point is to see the complexity of this view of religion. The complexity is linked to the fact that religion itself is a complex phenomenon not easy to understand. Truth in this area is often not obvious.

# PART 2

## A Defense

# 4

# Early Hinduism

A STUDY OF THE early stages of Hinduism will illustrate how different interpretations of the elements of religion can be found in the same religious tradition. We will also see how changes in interpreting elements one through four produce changes in interpreting element six.

Hinduism has its source in the religion of the early Indo-Aryans who came over the mountain passes in northwestern India about 1500 BCE. They then conquered the Indus Valley civilization. These Aryans were tall and fair skinned. They conquered Dravidians who were short and dark skinned.

What we know about these Aryans is found in collections of sacred writings, the early Vedas. The word "Veda" means knowledge—in this context, sacred knowledge. The earliest and most important of these writings is the Rig Veda, a collection of hymns (*mantra samhitas*). It is made up of ten books and 1028 hymns. These hymns, also referred to as prayers, are addressed to one or more the gods (*devas*) and used in rituals. There are three other collections of early Vedas which are dependent upon the Rig Veda, making four collections of early Vedas.

We will limit our discussion of Hinduism to an analysis of the Rig Veda and to two collections that followed them that followed them—the Brahmanas and the Upanishads. These two collections are added to each of the four collections of the early Vedas. In the broad use of the word, "Vedas" refers the early Vedas, the Brahmanas, and the Upanishads. In the narrow sense, it refers to the Rig Veda and the earliest material in the other three books.

The dating of these scriptures is difficult. The early Vedas, however, came upon the scene between about 1500 BCE and 900 BCE. The Brahmanas are dated around 800 BCE to 600 BCE. The Upanishads came upon the scene from about 600 BCE to about 300 BCE.

After the discussion of the early Vedas, Brahmanas, and the early Upanishads, we will examine and give a critique of how John Hick looks at these religious orientations.

## THE ELEMENTS IN THE EARLY VEDAS

If one peruses the hymns of the Rig Veda looking for emphases, one will find primacy being given to wealth, soma, and fighting. The moral law, *Rita*, is mentioned but not emphasized. It is often linked to the gods Varuna and Mitra, but also at times to Agni. References to life after death are very rare, even though there was such a belief. Belief in the transmigration of the soul is not found here.

These Aryans were concerned about this life, success in wealth, social status, and war. Indra is the ideal warrior. More hymns are addressed to him, about three hundred, than to any of the other gods. Rig Veda, book 2, hymn 12, says of him, "Without whose aid men conquer not in battle." This hymn then says, "Both heaven and earth, themselves, bow down before him: Before whose might the very mountains tremble; who, famed as Soma-drinker, armed with lightning, is wielder of the bolt: he, men, is Indra."

Soma drinker? It is said of Indra that he "was born to drink the Soma juice" (Rig 1.5). Soma was a fermented beverage given to the gods in rituals. "These juices are poured forth that gladden and exhilarate" (1.46). The whole of book 9 is devoted to the god Soma. Soma, however, was not limited to be used by the gods. "We have drank Soma and become immortal; we have attained the light the gods discovered. Now what may foeman's malice do to harm us?" (Rig 8.48)

Indra is also addressed this way: "To him the richest of the rich, the Lord of treasures excellent, Indra, with Soma juice outpoured. May he stand by us in our need and in the abundance for our wealth" (1.5). The phrase "abundance for our wealth" suggests that these rituals were for and sustained by the aristocrats—those who could afford rituals performed by priests. Indra is referred to as "the Treasure-Lord of wealth" (1.9). The god

Rita is referred to as the "Wealthier-giver." "May the Wealthier-giver grant to us riches that shall be far renowned" (1.15).

Agni is also an important god, mentioned in about two hundred hymns in the Rig Veda. He was identified with fire in general, particularly important in the elaborate sacrificial fires. He was also identified with the hearth fire in the home. The first hymn of the first book of the Rig Veda says, "Agni I praise, the household priest, Invoker, the best bestoweth wealth." Later in this hymn it says of him, "May he conduct us to the gods" and "Go straight, O Agni, to the gods." In other words, he was an intermediary between the ritual fire and the other gods. He is also referred to as "lord of the sacrifice" and "guardian of the Law."

The emphasis on pleasure, success and wealth is balanced by an emphasis on home, linked to Agni, and also to the moral law, linked to Indra and Varuna. According to hymn 61 in the seventh book these gods have avenging spies. It says, "Avenging spies pursue men's falsehoods closely; there are no secrets that ye [Varuna and Mitra] cannot fathom." This hymn then says, "Praise the law of Varuna and Mitra: Their force the two worlds keep with might asunder. The mouths of impious men shall pass by sonless. May those on worship bent increase their homestead."

When Hinduism developed in later years it came to recognize four permissible goals. The first two were pleasure (*Kama*) and success (*Artha*). These goals seem aimed to capture what the early Vedas emphasized. Pleasure was understood as related to the body and success was linked to wealth and social status. These are non-moral values. The third permissible goal was *dharma*, duty based upon law. This would include the moral law linked to Mitra and Varuna. We do not have any discourse explaining what that included in the early Vedas. When a god is recognized as honest and truthful, that gives us some insight as to what they had in mind. The fourth permissible goal is liberation (*moksa*). That is introduced later in the Upanishads.

The first element of religion includes beliefs and assumptions about values. For the Rig Veda this is captured in the first two permissible goals, pleasure and success.

The second element is beliefs and assumptions about finding life at its very best, i.e., spiritual hypotheticals. The early Aryans believed that happiness was best achieved by pleasures linked to the body and success in this world. However, there are no spiritual hypotheticals here. Much later, there are discussions of how to achieve pleasure and success. The paths, however, did not involve any reference to a god or any gods. Our interest is in those hypotheticals involving type six entities. How to succeed in business does not involve a spiritual hypothetical.

The third element of religion is beliefs and assumptions about human nature. This includes optimism verses pessimism as to what humans can achieve, and also views of what we are as human beings. The early Vedas clearly have an optimistic tone. They represent the aristocrats who have achieved much and believed that they can achieve more.

What about what we are as human beings? The emphasis is on the physical. We are physical beings. Even the gods are portrayed as having bodies and Indra is described as having a big tummy because of his love of Soma.

Beliefs and assumptions about rituals is the fourth element of religion. We find here some changes took place during the era of the early Vedas. The earliest rituals were fairly simple and forbade magic and sorcery. The rituals, however, became more elaborate and magic and sorcery is found in some of the late Rig Veda. The last of the early Vedas, the Atharva Veda, begins with a section on magical charms. This is followed by longer hymns involving speculation about the meaning of ritual. The concept developed that by controlling the sacrifice one could control the universe. This is what we find in the next set of scriptures, the Brahmanas.

The fifth element of religion involves beliefs about authority. There is no mention of authority within the early Vedas, but they eventually became part of the Vedas in the broad sense. This includes the early Vedas, the Brahmanas, and the Upanishads. These are the primary scriptures of Hinduism. To reject the Vedas is to reject the faith. Buddhism might have ended up being another form of Hinduism, but they rejected the Vedas and thus rejected the faith.

The sixth type of belief is belief about God, the gods and similar things. What can be said about them in the early Vedas? We can say that there were many gods which mostly reflected the primary values of the early Aryans—pleasure and success. That reflected the values of the more aristocratic early Aryans. That should surprise no one.

It is said of Indra, "Both heaven and earth, themselves, bow down before him" (2.12). The impression one gets is that he is being portrayed as above the other gods. This pattern of considering the god addressed as superior is referred to as henotheism.

## EARLY HINDUISM

In the last book of the Rig Veda, book 10, we find examples of speculation in the form of monism and monotheism. Monism is the view that ultimately what exists is one thing. In hymn 90, Parusha is a cosmic man who is regarded as the soul of the universe and the physical universe his body. "A thousand heads has Parusha, a thousand eyes, a thousand feet. . . . This Parusha is all that hath been and all that is to be." Hymns 121 and 129 are monotheistic.

Hymn 121 is a classic piece of monotheistic speculation:

> Non-being then existed not, nor being
> There was no air, nor sky that is beyond it . . .
> Death then existed not, nor life immortal . . .
> That which, becoming, by the void was covered,
> The One by force of heat came into being.
> Desire entered the One in the beginning:
> It was the earliest seed, of thought the product.
> The sage searching in their hearts with wisdom,
> Found out the bond of being in non-being.
> Who knows for certain? Who shall here declare it?
> Whence was it born, and whence came this creation?
> The gods were born after this world's creation.
> Then who can know from whence it has arisen?
> None know whence creation has arisen;
> And whether he has or has not produced it.
> He who surveys it in the highest heaven,
> He only knows, or haply he may know not.

When it was said that interpretations of the elements of life are important, it did not mean that speculation plays no role. Later we will find an example of speculation in the Upanishads.

## THE ELEMENTS IN THE BRAHMANAS

As mentioned above, the early Vedas were four collections of sacred writings. Collections of Brahmanas were added at the end of each of the early Vedas. Two Brahmanas were added to the Rig Veda.

These Brahmanas are detailed discussions of exactly how the rituals are to be performed. They focus on the meaning of the rituals, and on the creative power of the proper words and ritual acts. Rituals became a form of engineering. A link was drawn between the rituals and the larger universe. Microcosmic rituals were tied to a macrocosmic universe. The performance of the rituals came to be considered necessary to maintain order in the universe; the priests became more in important than the gods.

The values of the early Vedas did not change. Importance was still given to physical pleasure, and to success in wealth and in society. They were balanced off by an emphasis on the home and the moral law. There was also no difference with respect to the understanding of human nature. We are physical beings, and there was faith that life could be significantly improved.

At this point speculation started to develop in the following way. If the holy power present in the ritual could manipulate the universe, even its gods, might not this holy power be the central power of the universe?

## THE ELEMENTS IN THE EARLY UPANISHADS

An answer to our question is found in Kena Upanishad, part 1:

> What cannot be spoken with words, but that whereby words are spoken: know that alone to be Brahman, the Spirit; not what people here adore. What cannot be thought with the mind, but that whereby the mind can think: Know that alone to be Brahman, the Spirit; and not what people here adore. What cannot be seen with the eye, but that whereby the eye can see: Know that alone to be Brahman, the Spirit; and not what people here adore.

We have here a shift in the interpretation of the first element and the sixth element, which involves interpretations of God and the gods.

The Upanishads come after the early Vedas. "Not what people here adore" is a rejection of the values of the early Vedas. The Katha Upanishad, part 2, puts it succinctly: "There is the path of joy, and there is the path of pleasure. Both attract the soul. Who follows the first comes to good; who follows pleasure reaches not the end." In other words, in the short run pleasure may be great, but in the long run, the path of joy wins. Pleasure and pain are perceived as going together. If you have one you will get the other, and together they form a type of bondage from which to escape. The joy of the Spirit brings freedom.

Let's consider what this Brahman is, and what the path of joy is. Brahman is the ultimate power which enables us to speak and think. It is also something which cannot be spoken by words and cannot be thought with the mind. Brahman so conceived is referred to a Nirguna Brahman, God without attributes. Language and thought divides up the world. The ultimate reality here is the One without duality. The alternative is Saguna Brahman, Brahman with attributes. God is then perceived as personal. In some of the later Upanishads the ultimate is regarded as Saguna Brahman.

In the Chandogya Upanishad, a father gives his son a lesson. The son is given the fruit of a banyan tree and told to break it. He sees small seeds. The father tells the son to break a seed and then asks him, "What do you see?" The son answers, "Nothing." The father then says, "From the very essence in the seed which you cannot see comes in truth this vast Banyan tree. Believe me my son; an invisible and subtle essence is the Spirit of the whole universe. That is Atman. *Thou Art That*" (7.6). In other words, the son's true self is the Self of the Universe, Atman, which is Brahman.

To make sense of this one has to grant that there are different degrees of reality. One's highest self in the non-dual Atman/Brahman and the ordinary self is a manifestation of that higher self.

The other question is: What is the path of joy? How does one attain the joy the Spirit which is ever free? The Chandogya Upanishad says that one needs a master to direct him to the land of the Spirit. The method involves meditation. "Meditation is in truth higher than thought. The earth seems to rest in silent meditation . . . Whenever a man attains greatness on this earth, he has his reward according to his meditation" (7.6). By means of meditation one comes to contemplate the Infinite Spirit, one's true Self, and to find freedom of the Spirit and joy. The Infinite Spirit is also referred to as "the Spirit of peace" (Katha, part 3).

How does one recognize the Infinite Spirit? One is not conscious of any "thing." It is pure consciousness, pure awareness. The Brihad-Aranyaka Upanishad: "The supreme Spirit is an ocean of pure consciousness boundless and infinite" (2.4). It brings bliss, peace, and joy. It is also referred to as the Spirit of peace. This world is a manifestation of that Infinite Spirit, Atman/Brahman.

Not just any kind of meditation will lead one to know the Infinite Spirit. The meditation takes place in the context of the Brahman/Atman doctrine. The master must be one who has come to know Brahman.

According to the Kena Upanishad becoming aware of Brahman, our true self, happens in an experience of ecstasy. This is sometimes referred to as *moksa*.

## Part 2—A Defense

Moksa involves an experience of ecstasy, joy, and peace. It also plays a role in the larger scheme of things. The Katha Upanishad, part 3, says, "When consciousness of the Atman manifest itself, man becomes free from the jaws of death." It then says at one point that death itself is carried away. How can death be carried away? Here the belief in *samsara* is being assumed. This is the belief that the cycle of life followed by death, followed by life, followed by death, tends to go on endlessly.

The oddity here is that this belief is not found in the early Vedas or in the Brahmanas. It is also not introduced as a new doctrine in the Upanishads, but is just being assumed as true. The view could be the influence of the Dravidians who were in the Indus Valley before the Aryans arrived.

With the belief in samsara came also the belief in the law of karma. This is the belief that the way one lives in this life will determine how one is born in the next life. The gospel, or good news, of the Upanishads is that one can escape from the cycle of samsara. It happens by coming to know Brahman through the experience of moksa.

The doctrine of samsara introduces a type of metaphysical speculation which supplements its Brahman/Atman doctrine—which is a form of monism. Integrated into this speculation is a shift in the interpretation of the first four elements. There is a shift in values from an emphasis on pleasure and success to the importance of inner peace and joy—element one. We have the introduction of a spiritual hypothetical—element two. Happiness is best found through meditation by which one comes to know Brahman, one's true Self. For this one needs to work with one who has come to know Brahman.

The early Vedas are optimistic about finding happiness through physical pleasure and success in this world. The Upanishads reject this. The Upanishads are optimistic about finding happiness through meditation—element three. The early Vedas reject this. The early Vedas emphasize the physical. We are material beings. The Upanishads emphasize the spiritual. We are primarily spiritual beings—also element three.

What about element four—the priests and the rituals? One does not need a priest to meditate. They lose their status and importance. In the early Rig Veda the priests at first were not important and then increase in importance. In the Brahmans the priests eventually become more important than the gods because they could manipulate the universe. With importance being given to meditation in the Upanishads, the priests lose their status and importance.

The best way to understand this is to realize the early Vedas emphasized war, success in society, wealth, and enjoying soma and the pleasures of the flesh. What was added to this in the Brahmanas is the importance of the priests who considered themselves more important than the gods. A backlash to this was almost inevitable. There were too many drunken priests who thought too much of themselves.

The Upanishads introduced a countercultural movement analogous to the sixties. Not everyone bought into the movement. Everyone didn't leave the cities and go into the forest to meditate. They did not introduce changes to the social and economic structures of society. They rejected the society and its culture and introduced what was considered a higher form of life which led to inner peace and bliss.

## A CRITIQUE OF JOHN HICK

In the last chapter we described the views of John Hick. He says that Hinduism, Buddhism, Christianity, and Islam have a common structure which he calls soteriological. By this he means a transition from an unsatisfactory state to a "limitlessly better one." The transition is viewed as occurring by means of religious experiences. With respect to the Upanishads what he has in mind are the experiences of moksa, which are experiences found in meditation. With these experiences he wishes to say, "Salvation/liberation consists in a new and limitlessly better quality of existence which comes about in the transition from self-centeredness to Reality-centeredness."[1] As mentioned before, "better quality of existence" can refer to two different things. It can refer to finding happiness and well-being, as opposed to sorrow and suffering; or it can refer to embedding in one's life or the life of the society the best values.

Earlier it was mentioned that there have been a number of studies of people living in many different cities. They ask people the extent to which they find happiness. New York City does not usually come close to the top in these studies. A study then discovered that the awareness of suffering and problems in the world adversely affected their happiness index. Thus the value index of those living in New York might be higher than those found in some of the other cities, but their happiness index is lower. We thus have two indexes, a happiness index and a value index.

---

1. Hick, "On Grading Religions," 453.

## Part 2 — A Defense

Let's consider the happiness index first. Those who identify with the Upanishads do not deny that pleasure can be found through food, drink, and sex. They know also that success in this world can be a very appealing experience and a means to happiness. Neither would the defender of the early Vedas deny that inner peace and bliss can be found through meditation. The issue here is over which approach in the long run is the best approach to finding happiness and well-being. Here the Upanishads introduce a pessimistic view of human nature with respect to bodily pleasure. The search for bodily pleasures and success usually leads to pain, to hangovers and painful forms of conflict. Connected to this pessimism is an optimistic attitude as to what can be achieved by means of meditation. The emphasis here is on finding inner peace and bliss.

Every society has ways of determining who is successful. Parents want their children to find happiness. They often think of happiness as something found by achieving success in society. The Upanishads are a counter-cultural movement which pushed against that. It denies that true happiness can be found by emphasizing what society refers to as success.

The Upanishads did not capture the minds and hearts of everyone. A society requires economic, social, and political foundations that the Upanishads do not provide. There were and are arguments on both sides of this divide. In other words, to understand the kind of experiences Hick refers to, we have to put those experiences in their contexts and see that there is an argument here over how happiness and well-being can best be achieved.

The other factor is the value index. The question here is about which kind of person is the best model of what a person should be. Is it the person who is likely to be found in a cloister that enables him or her to focus on a life of meditation? Or is it the person whose life is focused on finding success, for example, in business or a trade? The Rig Veda emphasizes wealth, but societies sometimes recognize it in other ways. Success might be perceived as being a good fisherman or a skilled craftsman.

Besides a conflict over the understanding of the happiness index and the value index, there is also a conflict over metaphysics. The early Upanishads build into their religious view a speculative metaphysical system referred to as monism. The view is that ultimately what is real is one thing. Here it is Brahman/Atman. Things that we normally consider real, such as physical objects, are considered emanations from Brahman/Atman and have less reality. What reality they have comes from Atman/Brahman, and in a sense are aspects of Atman/Brahman. To make sense of this, one has to think in terms of entities having different degrees of reality. Matter has the least reality. The non-dual Atman/Brahman has the most. "Brahman" here has two senses. In one sense it is the non-dual One, and in the other sense it refers to everything including what emanates from it.

Beliefs and assumptions about human nature is one of the elements of religion. There is a prima facie problem embedded in this monism. We know that lack of oxygen to the brain results in an immediate loss of consciousness and damage to the brain significantly affects our mental life. In monism the less real cannot affect the more real because the less real emanates from what is more real. Consciousness is more real than body. Thus oxygen and brain states ought not to be able to affect mind and consciousness which are considered more real.

John Hick focuses on religious experiences linked to moksa and meditation. These religious experiences, however, need to be understood in the contexts of arguments related to the happiness index, the value index, and to metaphysics.

He can be credited with helping move the study of philosophy of religion from a study of classical theism to a study of religion. His suggestion that Hinduism has a soteriological structure is also helpful. What is lacking is a close enough analysis of what that soteriological structure is.

# 5

# Early Buddhism

BUDDHISM AROSE IN INDIA in the sixth century BCE. In that context belief in samsara, the law of karma, and the ideal of liberation permeated the religious landscape. Samsara is the belief that life is followed by death, followed by life, followed by death, endlessly. With this came the belief in the law of karma—how one lives in this life will determine how one is born in the next life. It will shape the character of one's next life. Liberation is escaping from the process of samsara and finding life at its very best.

The founder of Buddhism is Sakyamuni, sage of the Sakyas. He is known more by the name Gautama, which is the name of the tribe to which he was born. He was born about 560 BCE, a couple of hundred years after the early Upanishads started to appear. Mahavira, the founder of Jainism, was born about 600 BCE. Both were raised in families that were financially successful; both were dissatisfied with their lives. Both were interested in finding the best way to find liberation and life at its very best.

According to the Buddhist story, Gautama's father was warned at his birth that this son might become a wandering, homeless monk. He therefore sheltered him from the evils present in this world—old age, disease, and death. It then happened on one day that he sees an old man who is about to die from his infirmities; a sick man who was suffering from a high fever, and a corpse. He also sees a wandering monk in a yellow robe who had found true peace in his soul and freedom from the miseries of old age, disease, and death. He then decided to leave his home—his father, wife and child—and becomes a wandering monk. His goal was to find an answer to the problems that plague human existence and to find liberation. He went on a six-year quest studying with various teachers. This included an extreme form of asceticism when life almost left him.

After this six-year quest to achieve liberation, Gautama had a life-transforming experience. He achieved enlightenment, which is also described as achieving Nirvana. This enlightenment was a revelation because he learned the Truth, the Dharma, which became the basis of his preaching.

Within Buddhism between 100 BCE and 100 CE, a movement developed which referred to itself as *Mahayana*. This word meant Great Vehicle or Great Course. Members of this movement were, by implication, referring to those who were not a part of this movement as *Hinayana* (Inferior or small vehicle). Rather than use the pejorative term Hinayana, the alternative to Mahayana Buddhism is referred to as Theravada Buddhism. The scriptures that preceded this movement are called *Suttas* and were written in Pali. The new writings, which embellished on the earlier writings, are referred to as *Sutras* and written in Sanskrit. An understanding of these two traditions requires an understanding of their different interpretations of the elements of religion.

## THE ELEMENTS IN THERAVADA BUDDHISM

Among the elements of religion, two were not part of the dharma of early Buddhism—beliefs about rituals and beliefs about authority. This is not to say anything about practices. People have a tendency to recognize certain objects as holy and develop rituals related to those holy objects.

This rejection was a rejection of the rituals in the Brahmanas, a rejection of their priests, and a rejection of the authority of the Vedas. Since the rejection of a belief is itself a kind of belief, the Theravada Buddhists had beliefs relevant to these two elements. Their focus, however, was on the elements of life, the first three elements, and the sixth element—beliefs with respect to God, the gods, and similar kinds of "things."

### Element One: Values

In Gautama's enlightenment he learned the truth. It was also a transformative experience in which peace and bliss came to permeate his life. When he went out to preach, his former friends observed him and knew that he was a changed person. The emphasis on inner peace and bliss, not linked to the body or any of its functions, shows the presence of an ideal psychological state. It is analogous to what is found in the Upanishads. This was the supreme value in both traditions. The difference lies in Gautama's dharma.

His dharma involves what is called the Four Noble Truths. It is akin to psychotherapy because first an analysis of a patient's problem is given. This is followed by an explanation of the cause of the problem—the second truth. The patient is then told that by eliminating the cause, a cure can be found—the third truth. The patient is then given an outline of how the cause can be eliminated—a spiritual hypothetical which is the fourth truth.

In this case, the patient is all of us. We are in very bad shape. Our problem is that we have *dukkha* (sorrow, suffering). Birth is suffering; old age is suffering; sickness is suffering; death is suffering; despair is suffering; contact with unpleasant things is suffering; not getting what you want is suffering. The experienced world is suffering. In fact all existence as we know it is subject to dukkha; it is out of whack. Nothing is the way it should be.

This is not to suggest that life in this world is considered a living hell. This would suggest the appropriateness of an extreme form of asceticism.

We thus have two contrasting sets of values.

## Element Two: Spiritual Hypotheticals

Related to this value orientation is a spiritual hypothetical. The cause of dukkha is *tanha* (craving)—craving for pleasure, for existence, for coming to be, for nonexistence, for ceasing to be. Getting rid of tanha will bring us to life at its very best, peace and bliss, Nirvana. It is an ideal state of mind in which tanha is extinguished.

Achieving Nirvana also releases us from samsara. Everything in this world is subject to samsara. Even the heavens where the gods live belong to the realm of samsara. They are subject to dukkha and to the processes of samsara.

Finding release is referred to as moksa. Release from the realm of samsara and to find life at its very best involves a spiritual hypothetical— the Noble Eightfold Path. It extinguishes craving and brings peace and bliss. Here we do not have a set of particular steps like the twelve steps of Alcoholics Anonymous. What we have is an outline of a path that is best filled in by a teacher. A person serious about attaining liberation, attaining Nirvana, should join a sangha. A sangha is a monastic community that meets in the forest where one would learn from others the details of the path. The Eightfold Path involves right views, right intention, right speech, right action, right livelihood, right effort, right mindfulness, and right concentration. The last step involves a state of trance, which is a result of mental discipline that yields pure ecstasy and supra-consciousness.

## Element Three and Six

After death a perfected saint enters Final Nirvana, *Parinirvana*. We might call this Nirvana in its fullness. According to the scriptures the Buddha is asked whether such a person exists after death or does not exist; whether he both exists and does not exist, or neither exists and does not exist. The answer is that such categories do not apply. Existence and nonexistence apply only to conditioned things. The unconditioned transcends them.

Nirvana is the unconditioned ultimate—Theravada's interpretation of element six. To achieve and enter it is the ultimate goal of the Theravada monk.

Phrases such as "ultimate peace and bliss" are applied to Nirvana but one must keep in mind that they are metaphors. Edward Conze lists a number of words that are used: "permanent, stable, imperishable, immovable, ageless, deathless, unborn, and unbecoming."[1] The danger in using such words is to lose sight of the transcendence of Nirvana.

The last part is akin to what we find in the Upanishads. Gautama, however, not only denied the Brahman/Atman doctrine, he denied that there is such a thing as a self—that there is a substance making up a self. What constitutes self is a set of processes, material and mental forces referred to as *skandhas*. They are bodily form, feeling, conception, dispositions, and consciousness. They are all impermanent, changing processes that lack a self. This is an interpretation of element three.

This may sound strange, but it is analogous to a view that Gilbert Ryle takes in his *Concept of Mind*, a classic in linguistic philosophy. He says that the mind is not a mental thing, not a substance.

In promoting the Dharma, Buddhists emphasize two things. First, Gautama was only interested in practical things. According to the Upanishads when one is taught meditation by a master one begins with a metaphysical system. Gautama was more pragmatic. Whether or not the world

---

1. Conze, *Buddhism*, 40.

is eternal or not eternal; whether it is finite or infinite, he did not seek to explain.

The other point emphasized is that the Dharma avoids extremism. It rejects the extreme of bodily pleasure, found in the early Vedas; it also rejects the extreme of asceticism, taught by Mahavira, the founder of Jainism. Gautama taught a middle way.

Earlier the point was made that some individuals will place a greater value on physical pleasure and success, instead of the mental states of peace and bliss. There is an argument here. It is over which approach leads to our long-term well-being, that is, over a spiritual hypothetical. Some individuals will identify with the ideals of the early Vedas, pleasure and success; some will identify with the ideals of peace and bliss. That same argument arises here.

Gautama has one advantage over the views in the Upanishads. According to the Upanishads the body is dependent upon spirit or mind because it is a manifestation of Atman/Brahman. Consciousness and mind, however, are dependent on the brain. A lack of oxygen to the brain results in an immediate loss of consciousness. If we think of the brain as bodily form, then Gautama's view is compatible with this.

Assessing spiritual hypotheticals is going to be put off until the last chapters. In chapter 14 the views of John Bradshaw will be presented and discussed. Rather than emphasizing the extinguishing of attachment to the self, he thinks that attachment to self ought to be strengthened. He believes that suffering is often caused by a lack of love for self, a lack of self-esteem, which he says often leads to a sense of shame and suffering. We will put off that discussion until later.

## THE ELEMENTS IN MAHAYANA BUDDHISM

As mentioned above, between 100 BCE and 100 CE a movement developed which is referred to itself as Mahayana. This involved two shifts in values. For the Theravada Buddhist this world was permeated with sorrow and suffering. That disappears with Mahayana Buddhism. The other shift involves the ideal of love.

With the emphasis on love, Bodhisattvas become important. These are Buddhas-to-be who embody the ideal of love. Before he came to earth, Gautama was regarded as a Bodhisattva. Once Gautama came to earth, he was not a Bodhisattva. He was considered a Manushi Buddha known for

# Early Buddhism

his teaching. After death he was considered as having entered Final Nirvana and no longer important.

This world, however, became permeated with Bodhisattvas. They are ideal compassionate beings, heavenly beings portrayed in bright, multicolored clothing wearing silver and gold. What a difference between these beings and the Theravada monks who lived in the forest and lived by begging. Both the clothes and the emphasis on compassion reflect a significant change in values—element one. The Theravada monk had a duty to do good for others as he lived apart from the larger society, but the Bodhisattva identified himself with the normal concerns of people in society. People prayed to them for the sake of these concerns. Many Bodhisattvas were recognized. Particular groups focused on particular Bodhisattvas. Maitreya, Mansjusri, and Lord Avalokita are examples.

Here we see how a shift in values that led to a new interpretation of element six. This is what was said in chapter 3. A shift in interpretation of other elements leads to a shift in interpretation of element six. We saw this in the Hindu tradition where an emphasis in on inner peace and joy resulted in recognition of Brahman instead of the early Vedic gods. They represented pleasure and success.

Another type of Buddha figure that came upon the scene is the *Dhyani Buddhas*. Like Bodhisattvas, they are heavenly Buddhas to whom prayers are offered. The word *dhyana* implies that they are contemplative; rather than wear rich colorful garments, the Dhyani Buddhas are clothed in the simple garments of a monk. Like Bodhisattvas, there are many of them and particular groups focused on particular Dhyani Buddhas. Pure Land Buddhism recognizes Amida (or O-mi-to) and is known for its view that salvation is a matter of faith apart from meritorious works. With the rise in popularity of Bodhisattvas and Dhyani Buddhas, Gautama and Manushi Buddhas became less important.

Whereas most Mahayana Buddhists focus on Bodhisattvas or Dhyani Buddhas, there is a type of Buddhism that recognizes them but does not focus on them. This is Zen Buddhism. Rather than focusing on the Bodhisattvas or Dhyani Buddhas and praying to them, the emphasis is on discovering our Buddha-Nature. To discover our Buddha-Nature is to achieve Buddhahood, enlightenment. This enlightenment is not linked to something transcendent; nor is it linked to prayers to a Bodhisattva or to a Dhyani Buddha. The emphasis is on immanence of the Buddha-Body in all things. This world is a manifestation of the Buddha-Body.

## Part 2 — A Defense

For Zen the *Prajna-paramita sutrass* are important. The primary claim here is that the distinction between samsara (this world of transitoriness and transmigration) and Nirvana is empty, void. This is part of a broader view that language itself has difficulty in capturing the nature of reality. Doctrines are thus looked down upon. This, however, does not stop them from using the word "Nirvana." In fact, this world is referred to as Nirvana. "This is it!" is the way Alan Watts puts it.[2]

If language cannot capture the nature of reality, then Zen Buddhism would seem to conflict with the view of religion presented in this book. If language cannot capture the nature of reality, how then could Zen be regarded as having an interpretation of the elements of religion? This problem will be discussed in chapter 11. The focus will be on Rinzai Buddhism.

Since there are many forms of Mahayana Buddhism, there isn't just one interpretation of the elements. For most individuals, however, the ideal of love is affirmed. This ideal is embodied in the ideal of a Bodhisattva or a Dhyani Buddha. There is also is positive value given to life in this world. It was a shift in values that led to a shift in beliefs and assumptions about the gods, God, and Nirvana.

In chapter 12 a critique will be given of the interpretations of the elements of life to be found in early Buddhism. Chapter 11 will argue that interpretations of the elements of religion apply to Zen and a critique of those interpretations will be given.

## SUMMARY

It is not difficult to see that early Buddhism involves interpretations of elements one, two, three, and six. A shift in interpretation of element one then led to a shift in interpretation of element six.

Theravada Buddhism valued this world and everything in it negatively. Dukkha—sorrow, suffering, and impermanence—permeated everything. This dukkha is caused by attachment and craving. Remove the craving will remove the dukkha. The way to do that, the spiritual hypothetical, is by the Eightfold Noble Path.

In Mahayana Buddhism this world was no longer looked down upon. The ideal of compassion was introduced. With this was introduced Buddha types to take the place of Gautama—Bodhisattvas and Dhyani Buddhas. These figures embodied the ideal of compassion.

2. See Watts, *This Is It*.

## Early Buddhism

Many types of Buddha sects developed recognizing different Buddha figures. Zen was one type of Mahayana Buddha sect that did not emphasize a Bodhisattva or a Dhyani Buddha. It will be discussed in chapter 11.

# 6

# Biblical Judaism
## The Torah

THE JEWISH SCRIPTURES, CALLED the Tanak, consists of the Torah (the Pentateuch), the Prophets, and the Writings. Any close reading of the Torah will show that various sources were used in bringing these five books together. The same event is sometimes described more than once in different ways. For example, there are two creation stories—Genesis 1:1—2:4a and 2:4b–25. In one case plant life precedes human life, and in the other case plant life comes after human life. One has the name "Yahweh" for God. The story is like folklore in that God walks in a garden in the cool of the afternoon. The other has the name "Elohim" for God and has a more sophisticated portrait of creation.

Serious study of the sources of the Torah began in the eighteenth century. Eventually out of those discussions Julius Wellhausen (1844–1918) came up with what has become the standard view of the origins of the Torah based on four sources: J, E, P, and D. J represent the Yahwist; E the Elohist source; P the Priestly source. D refers to Deuteronomy which is regarded as an independent source. It is believed to be the book that King Josiah found in the temple (2 Kgs 22). It was the basis of the reforms he instituted. It is thus a source which stands by itself.

James King West brings Wellhausen's view up to date by giving the following dates as dates recognized by most scholars: the Jahwist source at about 950 BCE; the Elohist at about 750 BCE; the Deuteronomist source

## BIBLICAL JUDAISM

at about 650 BCE; and the Priestly source at about 550 BCE. When two sources are brought together, it is referred to as a redaction. The first redaction was JE and is dated about 700 BCE. The redaction JEP is dated soon after 550 BCE. JEPD is dated between 500 BCE and 400 BCE.[1]

Richard Friedman takes issue with this traditional Wellhausen view. He argues that P must have been written before D.[2] Dates are always disputable. Our concern, however, is not with dates, but with theology, with the interpretations of the elements of religion embedded in the sources.

Since there is more than one interpretation of the elements, Scripture cannot determine the proper interpretation. It is for the individual to determine the best interpretation. Scripture provides the field upon which the games of theology are played, but the field does not determine the conclusion of any particular game.

## VALUES IN THE FOUR SOURCES

The first element includes beliefs and assumptions about values. Values divide up into moral values and non-moral values.

Both the Yahwist source and the Priestly source have a creation story which emphasizes the goodness of the physical world. The Yahwist creation begins with a beautiful garden with good fruit and even gold and precious stones available. What more would you want? Some would say a mansion with streets of gold, but the Yahwist is more of a naturalist. It says of the physical world in poetic language what the Priestly writer says again and again in more abstract language: "it's good, it's good, it's good." These are non-moral values.

Neither Deuteronomy nor the Elohist have a creation story or anything similar. It wouldn't fit into Deuteronomy. The Elohist may have had one, and then had it crowded out when J and E were merged. It seems that these two sources assume what the other sources assert—that the physical world is good.

What about moral values? The Yahwist source is the earliest source. The Torah is known primarily as a book of laws, but the Yahwist has no laws. Laws place restrictions on human behavior, but they also tells something about the being who is portrayed as giving the laws. There are two

---

1. West, *Old Testament*, 66–67.
2. Friedman, *Who Wrote the Bible?*, 208.

statements of the Ten Commandments, one in the Elohist source and the other in Deuteronomy.

Two parts of the Yahwist story are very disturbing from a moral point of view: the election of Abraham (Gen 12:1–3), and its implications, and the particulars of the exodus story. Neither story is consistent with any kind of moral consideration. This is consistent with a lack of concern about laws and principles. In the Abraham story Yahweh is described as choosing Abraham and says that he will make of him a great and mighty nation. Through him, it says, all the nations of the earth will be blessed. Besides, his descendants are to be given the land of Canaan. This is the justification used for the story of invading Palestine and destroying city after city, as is described in book of Joshua.

Genesis 17:8 has Yahweh saying, "I will give to you and your descendants after you, the land of your sojourning, all the land of Canaan, for an everlasting possession; and I will be their God." Genesis 12:3 says, "I will make of you a great nation, and I will bless you, and make your name great, so that you will be a blessing. I will bless those who bless you, and him who curses you I will curse; and by you all the families of the earth will bless themselves." In other words, people will be blessed and cursed not on the basis of their merits, but on the basis of their treatment of the heirs of Abraham. It is hard to find a moral principle that fits this. We thus have built into the Yahwist religious tradition a type of nationalism, a form of nationalism that is still with us in this day and age. It is continuing to have an impact by conservative Jews and Christians in the political scene in the Middle East. The Palestinians, of course, reject the whole story. What kind of God would bless and curse people on the basis of their treatment of a particular people, the Israelites?

Consider the exodus story. It is in part a story of liberation from slavery. Anyone who focuses on liberation is likely to identify with this story as well as Lincoln's emancipation proclamation and the work of Martin Luther King. There are significant differences, however. Lincoln is known for the respect and kindness he showed toward those who lost the war, whereas the Yahwist tends to just eliminate the enemy. At one point God brings death to every Egyptian family. In the end he kills Pharaoh's entire army. Martin Luther King made nonviolence a part of his methodology.

Two kinds of consideration should be given in thinking about this story. One is the question of truth. Did something like what is described

## Biblical Judaism

here actually take place? The other question is the nature of the justification for what is described here as happening.

Exodus describes colossal events involving the loss of the army of Pharaoh, the entire population of Egypt being affected by plagues, and significant interactions between Moses and Pharaoh. If we look at Egyptian texts, however, there is no evidence that the Israelites ever were in Egypt. Those who seek to date the exodus usually place it between 1290 BCE and 1250 BCE. The first reference to the Israelite in Egyptian literature, however, is a royal inscription dated 1220 BCE that refers to a campaign in Canaan in which the Israelites are described as having been annihilated. This is the earliest reference to Israel outside of the Bible.

What are the implications of this empty pot? There is no agreement among scholars. It is not the function of this book to track down controversial historical issues. The theology embedded in the Yahwist material is what it is, irrespective of its link to history.

According to the exodus story, God calls the shots and directs what happens. This raises the question of the justification for what is described as having happened. Whenever the will of God is appealed to for determining or directing one's actions, the question is likely to arise as to why one should do the will of God. Some version of what is called the divine command theory is assumed. A conservative view of this is that one should do the will of God just because God willed it. This is the view of Karl Barth. God is considered free to command anything and his commanding something makes it right. The liberal view is that God embodies the most important moral ideals, such as goodness, justice and righteousness. One should do the will of God because he embodies these ideals.

Clearly in the exodus story a conservative view of the divine command theory is assumed. Yahweh tells Moses to tell Pharaoh what he commands. No reason is given. It is assumed that if Yahweh commanded it, it should be done. Yahweh then says that he will hardened Pharaoh's heart so that Pharaoh will not do what Moses says. Yahweh also says that he will multiply signs and wonders, which involved the plagues. Exodus 10:1–2 says, "I [shall] ... show these signs among them ... that you may tell in the hearing of your son and of your sons how I have made sport of the Egyptians and what signs I have done among them." Bringing plagues on the Egyptians is considered here part of a game. It is a sport that gives the children of Moses a story to tell of the mighty deeds of Yahweh. The lack of any historical justification for this story can function as a kind of solace. "Thank God that that did not happen." The Yahwist's earlier statement about justice and righteousness (Gen 18:19) gets lost here. The same source says, "The Lord [Yahweh] is a man of war; the Lord [Yahweh] is his name" (Exod 15:2).

Note that the dating of the Yahwist is about 950 BCE. The dating of David's and Solomon's monarchies are from about 1000 BCE to about 922 BCE. Clearly the Abraham and exodus stories give support to the power and status of the monarchy. They give it divine sanction. The same can be said about the second psalm. It says,

> "I have set my king on Zion, my holy hill." I will tell the decree of the Lord: He said to me, "You are my son, today I have begotten you. Ask of me, and I will make the nations your heritage and the ends of the earth your possession . . ." Now therefore, O kings, be wise; be warned, O rulers of the earth. Serve the Lord with fear and trembling; kiss his feet. (Ps 2:6–10)

This is recognized as a Davidic psalm. David is looked upon as specially anointed by God and as having a divine status. In the New Testament, authors took this verse out of context and applied it to Jesus. If seeing this psalm as applying to David seems strange, the reader needs to take into consideration the audience that the author was addressing. This was the tenth century BCE. Note also the phrase "he said to me" and the reference to nations.

By way of a summary, we can say that the Yahwist emphasized the goodness of the physical world, but had little regard for moral values. To say that religious views of life embody interpretations of values in general, and moral values in particular, is not to say that a positive attitude toward moral values is taken. Later we will see that this negative attitude toward moral values is emphasized in Zen.[3] The reasons here are different, however. In this case a conservative view of the divine command theory is assumed, and this is linked to nationalism. If David is God's anointed one and his kingdom supreme, then moral values and moral principles may not be emphasized. Nationalism overrides moral concerns. This shapes the interpretation of the sixth element.

In contrast to the Yahwist, the Elohist is a moralist. What is sometimes regarded as an early statement of the law is found in Exodus 20:22—23:9. Here we have three chapters with statements of the law that are moral in nature and discussions of situations where moral problems arise. This is not to suggest that they are consistent with modern moral standards. No

3. See chap. 11.

modern moralist will accept slavery, even though the slave here is to be released after six years. Respect is likely to be shown for the Elohist, however, when he says that you shall not wrong or oppress a stranger, and shall not afflict any widow or orphan (Exod 22:21–23). A reason is given for not oppressing a stranger in Exodus 23:9: "You know the heart of a stranger for you were strangers in the land of Egypt." What is implied here is a golden rule argument. It was wrong for the Egyptian to oppress you, and thus it is wrong for you to oppress them.

In discussing the Moses-Pharaoh conflict, we saw a very conservative version of the divine command theory being assumed. God is regarded as free to command anything, and his commanding something makes it right. In the Elohist chapters on law there is a logic as to what ought to be done. It makes a difference whether a killing is a matter of forethought or something that just happens in a fight over some problem. A person is considered responsible for his animals. If an ox gores a person or another ox, the owner is considered responsible for that. If a man seduces a virgin, he is obligated to marry her unless her parents reject him. He still has monetary responsibilities, however. Preceding these early laws are the Ten Commandments, which are in the first part of chapter 20 of Exodus. The first four commandments are uniquely religious in character and the other six are moral in nature. This is the earliest statement of the Ten Commandments.

If the moral dimension of life is important, then God is not free to command just anything. The conservative view of the divine command theory is rejected. Doing what is moral is prima facie doing the will of God.

With respect to moral values in Deuteronomy and the Priestly source, we find a mixed bag. They have things in common with both the amoral perspective of the Yahwist source and the moral perspective of the Elohist source. Both adopt the Abraham story and the exodus story with their moral baggage. They justify the story of invading Palestine and killing of men, women and children in city after city while at the same time keeping cattle for bounty (Josh 8 and 10). They also have laws that are moral in substance as is found in the Elohist source. Deuteronomy has a restatement of the Ten Commandments. Leviticus 19:33 says, "When a stranger sojourns with you in your land, you shall not do him wrong. The stranger who sojourns with you shall be to as the native among you, and you shall love him as yourself; for you were strangers in the land of Egypt." This goes beyond loving your neighbor as yourself. It involves loving the alien as yourself.

PART 2—A DEFENSE

What can be said about this inconsistency? First, when a tradition of religious nationalism is embedded within a society, it is very difficult to change. Second, there is a natural tendency to think of moral rules and principles as applicable within a society. It is a different kind of thing to consider them as relevant between states. If we consider the history of mankind, it is very difficult to find contexts where moral principles were considered important with respect to the relationship between states. In chapter 15 we will find Reinhold Niebuhr questioning whether personal moral principles are applicable between states. Third, in focusing upon the Torah we are not seeing the whole story, a complete picture. There is room for criticism of the Torah. We will have to look and see what the prophets had to say.

## SPIRITUAL HYPOTHETICALS IN THE FOUR SOURCES

The second element of religion involves spiritual hypotheticals—views of wherein is found the sources of life and well-being, and the sources of destruction and spiritual death. Near the end of Deuteronomy, Moses is described as saying, "See, I have set before you life and good, death and evil. If you obey the commandments of the Lord your God . . . then you shall live and multiply" (Deut 30:15–16). Repeating this theme, Moses says, "I have set before you life and death, blessing and curse; therefore choose life" (Deut 30:19).

What make these commandments the source of life or death? We find the following near the beginning of Deuteronomy: "What great nation is there that has statutes and ordinances so righteous as all this law which I set before you this day?" (Deut 4:8). Deuteronomy 4:6, referring to the law, says, "Keep them and do them; for that will be your wisdom and your understanding." If the laws embody righteousness and wisdom, that would be a good reason for the Israelite to follow them because of what they are, not just because they were commanded by God. If they are righteous and embody wisdom, then they could be the source of life and well-being. A spiritual hypothetical needs backing.

What makes a spiritual hypothetical possible here is that God and his commandments must have the appropriate qualities. With his conservative view of the divine command theory, the Yahwist does not provide the context for a spiritual hypothetical. The Elohist, with his focus on the primacy of moral values, provides the context. The problem is finding one there.

The Priestly source, like Deuteronomy, is a mixed bag. There is at least the possibility of spiritual hypotheticals there.

A critic at this point may raise the following objection: Let us suppose in the Abraham story God is portrayed as saying that if you do whatever I command, then you shall be given the land. You must first kill off the Palestinians in their cities on your way to Jerusalem. I will then see to it that you have the land, but you must continue to do whatever I command in order to keep the land. If you don't, you shall be punished. Is not this a spiritual hypothetical with a conservative view of the divine command theory?

This is a rewards and punishment game. The command itself has no value. A command is followed for the sake of a reward, for getting something one wants. Getting what you want is not necessarily beneficial to one's well-being or to one's society's well-being. It is thus not a spiritual hypothetical.

Is Deuteronomy just playing a rewards and punishment game? The problem with this is that Deuteronomy gives us the reason he thinks we should follow the law at the beginning of the book. As mentioned above, he exalts the law because it embodies righteousness and wisdom (Deut 4:6, 8). It could be, however, that Deuteronomy is inconsistent here. He could have both points of view.

## HUMAN NATURE IN THE FOUR SOURCES

The third element of religion refers to views of human nature. This refers to two types of things: views about what human beings can or cannot achieve by their efforts; and views about what we are as human beings. This is about whether we are physical things, mental or spiritual things, or a combination of both.

Let's consider the first sense. There are three relevant passages, two in the Yahwist source and one in Deuteronomy. According to the Yahwist source, the Noah story says, "The Lord saw that the wickedness of man was great in the earth, and that every imagination of the thoughts of his heart was only evil continually. And the Lord was sorry that he had man on the earth" (Gen 6:5–6). It is as if creation was an experiment that went bad and human beings didn't turn out the way Yahweh was hoping or expecting. Here again we see that the Yahwist has the instincts of a poet, not the mind of a theologian.

## Part 2 — A Defense

What does the garden of Eden story tell us about human nature? Scholars have different views. In the Jewish tradition the story is usually seen as human beings maturing. They come to be like God and know good and evil, something the birds of the air and the beasts of the fields do not achieve. For the Apostle Paul and for most Christians the story has been seen as a story about human beings falling into sin. Sin comes to dominate human life. This author is not going to try and arbitrate this dispute, but it is important to see that there are these two ways of interpreting the story.

In Deuteronomy, its view of human nature is linked to its spiritual hypotheticals. It claims that life and well-being for the Israelites is found through the law. It thus considers human nature and the law as compatible. We thus find the following: "For this commandment which I command you this day is not too hard for you, neither is it far off. It is not in heaven, that you should say, 'who will go up for us to heaven, and bring it to us?'... But the word is very near you; it is in your mouth and in your heart, so that you can do it" (Deut 30:11–14). In other words, there is a harmony between the law and human nature. This is necessary if human well-being is to be found in the law. It is this passage from Deuteronomy that the Apostle Paul misuses and applies to the Christian gospel (Rom 10:6–7). For him the law brought spiritual death (Rom 7:9). The harmony he saw was between the gospel and human nature, not the law.

What does the Torah say about what we are as human beings? In the Eden story Yahweh forms man out of dust and breathes into his nostrils the breath of life (Gen 2:7). Emphasis: the physical nature of human existence. This rejects body-soul dualism, and also rejects the notion that we are spiritual beings. According to the latter what is called "matter" is really a manifestation of spirit. This is the only explicit view of what we are as human beings in the Torah.

Nothing in the other sources of the Jewish Bible conflicts with this point of view. The materialism of the Torah is at least one reason these Scriptures do not show any interest in life after death. There is always a tendency for people to read their own point of view into Scripture. The notion of life after death is important in the contemporary religious scene. It is thus important to keep in mind that this notion was not emphasized in the Torah.

## RITUALS IN THE FOUR SOURCES

The fourth element of religion refers to beliefs about rituals and their importance. Early in the Torah they were not important. The Yahwist does not present Yahweh as giving any laws as we find in the other sources. We find, however, burnt offerings being offered to God. After the flood Noah is described as taking every clean animal and bird, and then puts them as burnt offerings on an altar for God (Gen 8:20). Yahweh is described as smelling them and being pleased by their odor. Anybody who walks in the garden in the cool of the evening is likely to have a nose to smell things. Let's remember that the Yahwist has the instincts of a poet.

In Deuteronomy, Levitical priests become important. Sacrifices are to be performed by them (Deut 18:1–5). Deuteronomy 17:12 says, "The man who acts presumptuously, by not obeying the priest who stands to minister there before the Lord your God, or the judge, that man shall die." If the emphasis is on "justice alone" (Deut 6:20), then it is hard to see how disobeying a priest should result in death. In the Priestly source the rituals become more important and more elaborate.

If we look at the Torah as a whole, what can be said about the laws relating to rituals? What about the role and function of the priests? Wellhausen recognized three stages in the development of the priests. At first there were no fixed or hereditary priests. The second stage was in the age of the kings when Levitical priests emerged and became a dominant force. The final stage came after Babylonian captivity when there was a theocracy and the Aaronides ruled.[4] The early history of Israel is thus a history of the rise and power of the priesthood. In Leviticus, we find a lengthy elaboration of the various kinds of sacrifices that are appropriate for various kinds of occasions. In addition we have a discussion of holy days and food regulations. In other words, over time the priests became more powerful and centralized, and life became much more controlled by laws and regulations. We saw a similar development in the movement from the early Vedas to the Brahmanas.

## AUTHORITY AND GOD IN THE FOUR SOURCES

The fifth and six elements of religion involve beliefs and assumptions about authority and God, the gods, and similar "things." The early Vedas were not

---

4. Cross, *Canaanite Myth*, 194.

seen as have any authority, but they eventually came to be recognized as having authority. A similar thing can be said about the Torah. The Torah itself does not claim to be a revelation from God, but the law is looked upon as having come from God and carries his authority. The Torah itself does eventually come to have authority as the canon of the Hebrew Bible developed.

With respect to the sixth element we have the God of the Yahwist who takes a walk in a garden in the cool of the afternoon and who enjoys the smell of sacrifices. We also have the more sophisticated notion of God in the Genesis 1 creation story. Important in understanding God is how a person interprets the divine command theory. There are those who will identify with a conservative view in the tradition of Karl Barth, and those who identify with a more liberal view. The conservative view is consistent with God commanding all kinds of moral atrocities. The liberal view says that one should do the will of God because of the ideals he embodies. This would be consistent with the Elohist.

Anyone who identifies with the Torah would have a view of the religious ultimate that is consistent with the view of both creation stories—that the physical world is good. Much later that view of the physical world was rejected and the God of the Torah was demoted. This is found in Gnosticism.

## SUMMARY

There are many different interpretations of the elements of religion in the Torah. There is no simple progression which takes place over time. The Elohist which focuses on moral values comes after the Yahwist, the earliest of the sources. To understand the Elohist it helps to realize that it came out of the northern area of Israel, the context where Amos functioned. Amos also emphasized moral principles.

Both creations stories emphasized the goodness of the material world—a non-moral value.

The only spiritual hypotheticals we found were in Deuteronomy. They were linked to the fact that the law embodies righteousness and wisdom. The Elohist and the Priestly source could have spiritual hypotheticals, but do not seem to have any.

Deuteronomy has an explicit view of human nature to support its spiritual hypotheticals. If life is going to found in the law, then compatibility between law and human nature is important. The other sources seem to agree with this.

With respect to understanding what we are as human beings, the Yahwist makes explicit that we are material beings. The other sources seem to assume this. This is why there is no recognition of life after death in the Torah.

With respect to rituals and priests, we saw that they were not emphasized in the Yahwist. In the Priestly source religion became centered in the priests and their rituals.

With respect to authority we saw that the law is recognized as having come from God and as carrying the authority of God. The Torah itself, however, is not regarded as a revelation from God. It came to have authority when the Jewish canon took shape and form.

With respect to interpreting the sixth element three things are appropriate. There are two creation stories which emphasized the goodness of the material world. We have a very anthropomorphic God in the Yahwist creation story and a more sophisticated one in the priestly story. There are two views of the divine command theory. In the Yahwist account God seems free to command whatever he wants and his commanding something makes it right. When moral values are emphasized, then God is not free to command just anything. The view is that one should do the will of God because of the values he embodies. The Elohist was the source that emphasized moral values the most, but they can be found in Deuteronomy and the Priestly source. Deuteronomy says that God's law embodies righteousness and wisdom and thus considers the law as a source of life and well-being.

# 7

# Biblical Judaism
## Amos and the Prophets

THE PRESENCE OF PROPHETS and the practice of prophecy preceded the early prophets of Israel by at least a thousand years. The common view is that the prophets made ecstatic utterances that had a cultural and religious role, but contained nothing of any significant substance. This is not the case with respect to the Hebrew prophets. Their message sometimes sounds like fire and brimstone preaching, but the substance of what is said sometimes reflects what might be said by a contemporary religious liberal. We will see in chapter 14 that Walter Rauschenbusch, a liberal reformer, begins his famous book on social Christianity by describing the message of the prophets. He also considered these prophets as providing the background for understanding the figure of Jesus.

The message of these prophets took the form of poetry that was proclaimed orally in public locations, such as a court of a temple, a shrine, a city gate, or even a prison. In other words they were addressed to society, the general public. The step between being proclaimed orally and being found in a book remains largely unknown. However, Jeremiah tells us that he dictated oracles to the scribe Baruch (36:4), and Isaiah says that God told him to "write on a tablet and inscribe in a book" (30:8).

The phrase "Former Prophets" refers to a set of books which give a portrait of the life of the Israelites from the death of Moses to the fall of Jerusalem in 587 BCE. These books, which are by nature historical, include

Joshua, Judges, Samuel, and Kings. The phrase "Latter Prophets" refers not to just a set of books, but to a group of individuals each of which has their name on a book. They include Isaiah, Jeremiah, Ezekiel, and a group of individuals with small books referred to as "the Twelve."

The most important of the twelve prophets was Amos, an early prophet (ca. 750 BCE). He is important because he seemed to have influenced much of the message in other prophets, such as Isaiah and Jeremiah. We are going to focus on him, and then point to places where other prophets picked up his message.

## ELEMENT ONE: VALUES

Amos made his proclamations during the reign of Jeroboam of Israel (786–746 BCE). It was a peaceful time for Israel when foreign trade and business prospered. For him, however, prosperity was not a sign of God's blessing. For him the body was healthy, but the soul of Israel was corrupt. He says,

> Woe to those who lie upon beds of ivory, and stretch themselves upon their couches, and eat lambs from the flock and calves from the midst of the stall; who sing idle songs to the sound of the harp, and like David invent for themselves instruments of music; who drink wine in bowls, and anoint themselves with the finest oils, but are not grieved over the ruin of Joseph. (Amos 6:4–7)

The ruin of Joseph refers to the degradation of Israel. Jeremiah makes this same kind of point. He said,

> "Woe to him who builds his house by unrighteousness, and his upper rooms by injustice; who makes his neighbor serve for nothing, and does not give him his wages; who says, 'I will build myself a great house with spacious upper rooms,' and cuts out windows for it, paneling it with cedar, and painting it with vermillion. Do you think you are a king because you compete in cedar? Did not your father eat and drink and do justice and righteousness? Then it was well with him. He judged the cause of the poor and needy; then it was well with him. Is not this to know me?" says the Lord. (Jer 22:13–16)

This is an interesting view of religious knowledge. It is to embed in one's life God's will. Here it is to do justice and righteousness, and identify with the cause of the poor and needy.

## Part 2 — A Defense

The primary values for the prophets were moral values. The common way of emphasizing them was to emphasize justice and righteousness. Amos says, "Let justice roll down like waters, and righteousness like an ever flowing stream" (Amos 5:24). Hosea draws an analogy between Israel and God and a marriage relationship. Of Israel he has God say, "I will betroth you to me in righteousness and in justice, in steadfast love, and in mercy" (Hos 2:19). Referring to Israel, Isaiah has God say, "How the faithful city has become a harlot, she that was full of justice! Righteousness was lodged in her, but now murderers" (Isa 1:21). Micah is in this tradition when he says, "What does the Lord require of you, but to do justice, and to love kindness, and to walk humbly with your God" (Mic 6:8).

What doing justice and righteousness meant to them can be seen by looking at the specific things they emphasized. In the passage quoted above, Jeremiah links justice and righteous to judging the cause of the poor and needy. Isaiah says, "Seek justice, correct oppression; defend the fatherless, plead for the widow" (Isa 1:17). For Amos injustice was trampling on the weakest and most vulnerable. He says of his people, "They trample the head of the poor into the dust of the earth, and turn aside the way of the afflicted" (2:7). They "oppress the poor . . . crush the needy" (4:1). They "trample upon the needy, and bring the poor of the land to an end" (8:4).

Besides justice and righteousness, Amos emphasized doing good. "Seek good, and not evil that you may live . . . Hate evil, and love good, and establish justice in the gate" (Amos 5:14–15). Hosea emphasizes love. He has God say, "I desire steadfast love, and not sacrifice, the knowledge of God, rather than burnt offerings" (Hos 6:6). To which he adds, "Hold to love and justice" (Hos 12:6). Isaiah has a vision of the future without war. He says, "They shall beat their swords into plowshares, and the spears into pruning hooks; nation shall not lift up sword against nation, neither shall they learn war any more" (2:10). The whole of chapter 4 of Micah has this emphasis. What a contrast between this and the Yahwist who glorifies war and refers to God as a God of war.

Since the primary values were moral values, they assumed what was referred to earlier as a liberal view of the divine command theory. People ought to do what God commands because God embodies the ideals of justice, righteousness, and goodness. Jeremiah said, "Let him who glories glory in this, that he understands and knows me, that I am the Lord who practice kindness, justice, and righteousness in this earth; for in these thing I delight, says the Lord" (Jer 9:24).

We saw that Deuteronomy and the Priestly source emphasized the importance of justice, but then endorsed the Yahwist exodus story where the treatment of the Egyptians and the Pharaoh lacked any appropriate moral justification. Amos has an interesting twist here. It says, "'Are you not like the Ethiopians to me, O people of Israel?' says the Lord. 'Did I not bring up Israel from the land of Egypt, the Philistines from Caphtor and the Syrians from Kir?'" (9:7). The message here is that God loves the Israelites even as he loves the Ethiopians. What a deflation of the ego of the Israelites. It then says that he liberated not just the Israelites but also the Philistines and Syrians.

Here we see the egalitarian dimension of Amos. The message of the Yahwist was that God would bless nations on the basis of how they treated the Israelites. The message here is that God loves various peoples and is the liberator of various peoples, including the Israelites.

In these prophets we have a shift in element one and six of the elements of religion. The Yahwist emphasized war and nationalism. These prophets focused on justice, righteousness, goodness and peace. The Yahwist had a conservative view of the divine command theory. These prophets had a liberal view. The conservative says that one should do the will of God because God commanded it. The liberal says that one should do the will of God because God embodies the most important values.

What about non-moral values? We saw that the Yahwist has the story of man as beginning with an ideal garden. Consistent with this we have in the last chapter of Amos a portrait of an ideal future in which "mountains shall drip sweet wine, and all the hills shall flow with it . . . They [the Israelites] shall plant vineyards and drink their wine and they shall make gardens and eat their fruit" (9:13–14).

## ELEMENT TWO: SPIRITUAL HYPOTHETICALS

The second element of religion involves beliefs and assumptions involving spiritual hypotheticals. When there is a liberal view of the divine command theory, then there exists the possibility of spiritual hypotheticals because God embodies the appropriate values to bring life and well-being. It is thus significant that we find that Amos has God saying, "Seek me and live" (5:4), and says, "Seek the Lord and live" (5:6). It also says, "Seek good, and not evil, that you may live" (5:14). Social justice, righteousness, and goodness are seen as sources of life and well-being for the society.

Jeremiah says of the Israelites, "[They] went after worthlessness and became worthless? . . . For my people have committed two evils; they have forsaken me, the fountain of living waters, and hewed out cisterns for them themselves, broken cisterns that can hold no water" (Jer 2:5, 13). The life of the people lies in embodying in the society God's will and purposes; to embody in society the ideals of justice, righteousness, and goodness.

What does Isaiah mean when he says, "Zion shall be redeemed by justice and those who repent, by righteousness" (1:27)? To be redeemed is to find life, well-being. The life of the society for Isaiah is found through righteousness and justice.

## ELEMENTS THREE AND FOUR

The third element of religion is views of human nature. Is there any view of human nature in Amos? Deuteronomy spoke of how easy the law and how it conformed to human nature. We do not find that here. We also do not find here any cynicism. In Amos there is no assumption that the life of Israel will inevitably go down the drain. "Seek me and live" makes the assumption that the finding of life is possible. The same can be said about Jeremiah. He assumes that it is possible that his audience could return to the fountain of living waters that they had left.

The fourth element involves views about rituals. What do we find in Amos? Amos 5:21–25 reads as follows:

> I hate and despise your feasts, and I take no delight in your solemn assemblies. Even though you offer me your burnt offerings and cereal offerings, I will not accept them . . . Take away the noise of your songs . . . But let justice roll down like waters, and righteousness like an everflowing stream. Did you bring to me sacrifices and offerings the forty years in the wilderness, O house of Israel?

The answer to the latter question, of course, is, "No."

Jeremiah makes this same kind of point. He says, "For in the day that I brought them out of the land of Egypt, I did not speak to your fathers or command them concerning offerings and sacrifices" (7:25). To this Jeremiah adds, "Your burnt offerings are not acceptable, nor you sacrifices pleasing to me" (Jer 6:20). Isaiah says, "I have had enough of burnt offerings of rams and the fat of fed beasts; I do not delight in blood of bulls, or of lambs, or of he-goats" (Isa 1:1). Hosea has God say, "I desire steadfast love, not sacrifice, the knowledge of God, rather than burnt offerings" (Hos 6:6).

Some scholars believe that this is hyperbole. They believe that Amos did not want to do away with priests and the whole system of sacrifices.[1] Obviously there were some who took it literally. The fiftieth psalm has God say, "I will accept no bull from your house, nor he goat from your folds. For every beast of the forest is mine . . . Do I eat the flesh of bulls, or drink the blood of goats? Offer to God a sacrifice of thanksgiving" (50:9–14).

## ELEMENTS FIVE AND SIX

The fifth element refers to beliefs and assumptions about authority. Amos 2:4 has God saying, "I will not revoke the punishment: because they have rejected the law of the Lord, and have not kept his statutes." Both Isaiah and Jeremiah on numerous occasions have God condemning people for not keeping his law. The assumption is that God's law carries authority.

The sixth element involves beliefs and assumptions about God, the gods, and similar kinds of "things." Interpretations of elements one and two affect the interpretation of element six. With a liberal interpretation of the divine command theory God is perceived as embodying the highest moral ideals. These prophets also accepted the values embedded in the two creation stories—the view that the physical world is good and something to be enjoyed. Amos said that eventually "the mountains shall drip sweet wine, and the hill shall flow with it" (6:13).

When there are spiritual hypotheticals then the religious ultimate is seen as embodying important values and as the source of life. Interpretations of elements one, two, and six are tied together. In the prophets such as Amos, Isaiah and Jeremiah, God is seen as embodying the most important values and as the source of life and well-being.

## SUMMARY

The view in this book is that religious views of life change over time and they change based on reinterpretations of the elements of religion. We have seen in the Torah how a reinterpretation of the first four elements resulted in a change in the interpretation of element six. Let's trace what we have covered.

---

1. West, *Introduction to the Old Testament*, 302.

## Part 2 — A Defense

In the Yahwist account in the Torah we find a form of nationalism which says that God's will reward people not on the basis of fundamental principles, but on how they treat the Israelites. We also found an emphasis on war—a justification for killing men, women, and children as the Israelites go into the land of Canaan and destroy city after city. This is analogous to the early Vedas where the most important god, Indra, is a god of war without whom one conquers not in battle. Both also have an emphasis on the importance of this world and success within it. The biblical tradition differed in that it had an emphasis on nationalism.

In the early biblical tradition the priests start off not being very important. This is the Yahwist source. In the Priestly source, the last source of the Torah, religion is centered in priests and their rituals. The same thing happened in the Vedic tradition. The priests gradually increase in importance until they become more important than the gods in the Brahmanas.

In the biblical tradition, prophets such as Amos, Isaiah, and Hosea attacked the priests and their sacrifices; they emphasized instead the importance of justice and righteousness. In the Vedic tradition the status of the priests gets undermined with importance being given to Brahman and to meditation and finding inner peace and bliss.

In the biblical tradition, the understanding of the sixth element comes to embody the most important values—justice and righteousness. In the Vedic tradition, Brahman comes to be seen as embodying the most important values—inner peace and bliss. Let's recall what the traditional liberal view of religion says about these differences (see chap. 1.) From that perspective religious views of life have their roots in religious experiences of the same religious ultimate. The differences are due to culture. That means that the difference between the importance of inner peace and bliss, one the one hand, and justice and righteousness, on the other hand, is cultural. This is difficult to fathom. What it says to both traditions, however, is that what you consider important is it to a great extent a matter of culture. Don't take it too seriously. A certain kind of elitism is being assumed.

In both traditions when the religious ultimate is seen as embodying the most important values, then the role and the status of the priest gets undermined as well as earlier values. In the prophets, the importance of the priests and rituals gets undermined and then the importance of war. Focus is placed on justice and righteousness. In the Upanishads the importance of the priests gets undermined and then the importance of pleasure, success, and war. Emphasis is placed on meditation and finding inner peace and bliss.

In both traditions a spiritual hypothetical is introduced which enables one to know or properly relate to the religious ultimate and to find life and well-being. In the prophets, to know God or to embody his will and purposes in life is to find life and well-being. In the Upanishads, to know Brahman is to become aware of Brahman and to find inner peace and bliss and to know life at its very best. They differ in that the prophets focused on and addressed the society. The Upanishads focused on the individual person.

# 8

# Early Christianity
## Paul and the Book of Acts

IN OUR ANALYSIS OF religious traditions, we have started with the earliest scriptures, and then described changes as they came upon the scene. We saw how the religious tradition changed over time with the introduction of new scriptures. Interpretations of the elements of religion were the key to understanding those changes. The oddity in the New Testament is that the writings that focus on the life and teachings of Jesus, the gospels, come after the writings of Paul. He tells us nothings about the life and teachings of Jesus. The Lord's Supper, his death and his resurrection are mentioned. Christ's execution is dated around 30 CE. Paul's conversion is dated three to five years later. His first letter was written about twenty years after the execution. (I'm relying on Marcus Borg's dating.) After his conversion, Paul tells us that he did not go to Jerusalem to those who knew Jesus in the flesh (Gal 1:16–17). According to Galatians, after his conversion he went to Arabia. Three years later he was in Jerusalem for fifteen days. He visited Cephas (Peter) and met James, the brother of Jesus.

Fourteen years later, he says, he spent some time in Jerusalem and explained the gospel that he had been preaching. Paul makes it clear his message was controversial. "False brethren," he said, "were secretly brought in to spy on him" (Gal 2:4). Eventually, however, he said that he made peace with some of the leaders who extended to him the right hand of fellowship. It included James (the brother of Jesus), Cephas (Peter), and John (Gal 2:9).

# EARLY CHRISTIANITY

In the twenty-first chapter of Acts we are told of a later occasion when Paul was in Jerusalem. There James, the elders, and thousands of believers are described as taking issue with Paul's interpretation of the gospel. Acts tells us that the believers in Jerusalem were "zealous for the law" (Acts 21:20).

We are going to examine in some detail Paul's view of the gospel as it is found in Romans. We will then examine that view through the prism of the elements of religion.

According to Borg, Paul's letters are dated in the 50s. Mark, the first gospel, is dated about 70 CE; Matthew in the 80s. Traditionally, Luke's gospel has been dated in the 80s, but Borg has some persuasive arguments to put it in the first two decades of the second century. Luke is part of a two-part set—the book of Acts being the second part. Acts is important because it gives us a portrait of the Christian movement from its very beginning. It ends with Paul in Rome thirty-two chapters later. Paul's conversion experience is in chapter 8. Starting with chapter 13 the book focuses almost exclusively on Paul.

Unfortunately, we do not have anything from Peter, or anyone who knew Jesus in the flesh telling us their interpretation of the gospel. The earliest of the gospels, Mark, comes about forty years after the death of Jesus.

Two things are odd about Paul: his lack of interest in the historical Jesus, in consulting those who knew Jesus in the flesh; and his claim to be an apostle. At the beginning of each letter he refers to himself an apostle of Jesus Christ. In Luke 6:22, Jesus calls his disciples together, and among them chose twelve whom he named apostles. The author of Luke, who we will call Luke, then gives their names. Luke is also the author of Acts. The latter part of Acts, starting with chapter 13, focuses on Paul but never refers to him as an apostle. The only backing for Paul to have that title appears to be Paul himself. Paul appeals to his religious experience on the road to Damascus (Acts 9:3–19) to justify the title of apostle. The author of Acts recognized the religious experience, but never gave him the title. Nothing like the description found in Acts, however, is given by Paul. A study of Acts will reveal that in it nothing important happens without being a miracle.

The larger issue is whether or not the things that Jesus said and did are important to the understanding of gospel. This is not the context to try to resolve this problem. When scholars sort through this material, they often end up in one of two camps. Some say that Christian faith should be considered as a religion about Jesus, in the tradition of Paul; others say that it should be considered the religion of Jesus, in the tradition of Matthew,

Mark and Luke. Those who think of it as about Jesus focus on his death and resurrection, as Paul does; those who consider it to be the religion of Jesus focus on the things that Jesus said and did, as in the Synoptic Gospels.

We are going to begin with Paul's view of the gospel in Romans, which is the earliest statement of a gospel that we have. Acts comes at least thirty years later, and Borg would have us believe fifty to sixty years later. The question thus arises as to whether the portrait of Paul in Acts conforms to Romans. To answer that question will be our second project. In the first half of Acts Peter is the main figure. Galatians has Peter as a principal figure in the church in Jerusalem and, of course, each of the gospels emphasizes his importance. Our third task will be to examine the first half of Acts and the way that Peter is portrayed there—including his view of the gospel. His portrait will then be compared to Paul's portrait and the Paul's view of the gospel in Romans. The study of the gospels will be put off until chapter 9.

## THE GOSPEL IN ROMANS

Our study of Paul's view of the gospel is going to be limited to what is found in his Letter to the Romans. In the list of Paul's letters in the New Testament, this one comes first. It is recognized as his most important statement of the gospel. When Karl Barth wanted to emphasize the importance of Paul's theology, he chose to write a commentary on Romans. It is this author's belief that Paul changed his theology over time, but it would be beyond the scope of this chapter to track down those changes and give a complete picture of what Paul has written. Later we are going to be concerned about the influence that Paul's views have had. That influence is based on interpretations of the gospel found in Romans.

Gospel means good news. From an interpretation of the gospel one would thus expect to find a view of how human well-being and happiness can be found. We will find, however, that this is not the case for all interpretations of what Paul meant.

Briefly, the gospel for Paul in Romans is the claim that God sent his Son into the world to save us. Salvation comes by faith, apart from works of the law.

How Paul's view of the gospel is to be understood is controversial. In chapter 12 we will see that O. Hobart Mowrer is critical of Paul's views. His criticism is based, of course, on a particular way of interpreting Paul. Marcus Borg is a popular contemporary biblical scholar who is critical of how Paul is often interpreted. That includes the way Mowrer interprets him. How Paul is interpreted is thus a matter of controversy.

Eventually we are going to look at Paul's view of the gospel through then lens of the elements of religion. First, we are going to address the issue of how Paul is to be interpreted by considering what Borg has to say on the subject.

## BORG ON INTERPRETING PAUL

The understanding of faith and salvation is an important issue in the Lutheran tradition. Pietism arose in the Lutheran tradition due to the tendency to emphasize doctrine as opposed to religious experience. To use other language we could put it this way. There was a tendency to emphasize the metaphysical as opposed to the existential—people's lives and experiences.

Marcus Borg is concerned about the meaning of the words "redemption," "salvation," "justification," and "faith" as they are found in Paul's letters.[1] He says that there is a common practice of equating faith with belief, and then interpreting the other words entirely metaphysically, i.e., not linked to our lives and experiences. They interpret salvation, justification and redemption as getting into heaven. The concept of gospel then comes to refer to a way of making it into heaven. No spiritual hypothetical would be involved; no transformation of life would be involved. Spiritual hypotheticals involve experiences in this life, not in an afterlife. One way to put it is that salvation becomes primarily a metaphysical thing not linked to people's lives and experiences.

Believing, as Borg notes, involves propositions. His view is that the primary meanings of the word for faith were loyalty and trust.[2] Salvation, redemption, and justification involved, he says, a transformation of life. Using the language of the elements of religion, we can say that what Borg is saying is that for Paul salvation, redemption, and justification involve the value dimension of life. Life is transformed, made better, when one is saved.

What did Paul mean by faith? The best approach is to look what is said and the context in which it is said. Different contexts may have some differences in meaning. If we look near the beginning of Romans, we find Paul say that their faith "is being proclaimed in all of the world" (Rom 1:8).

1. Borg, *Evolution*, 119.
2. Ibid., 123.

When the significance of people's faith is applauded, it would not be their belief itself that is being applauded. Would it be trust? More likely, it seems to me, it would be their passionate commitment.

Near the end of the book, chapter 14, there is a discussion over the fact that some people believe that only vegetables should be eaten and some believe that anything can be eaten (Rom 14:2). Sounds like a contemporary discussion. Some believe that certain days ought to be observed to honor the Lord, and some don't. What is important, Paul says, is that whichever is done, it should be done unto the Lord. People ought not to judge. "For the kingdom of God does not mean food and drink but righteousness and peace and joy in the Holy Spirit" (Rom 14:17). Note that he does not make the kingdom a transformation of this world, but something spiritual. Note also Paul is saying something about his values—righteousness, peace and joy.

After saying that the issue of days and food are not important, he says that what is important is that whatever is done is done to honor the Lord. What is important is faith. Paul says, "He who has doubts is condemned, if he eats because he does not act from faith; for whatever does not proceed from faith is sin" (Rom 14:23). The opposite of faith here is doubt, not disbelief. The word "trust" fits here. In both of these cases, however, faith seems to involve a commitment.

In the middle of Romans it appears that there might be a problem. In chapter 4 he introduces the importance of faith by referring to Abraham. He refers to Genesis and says of that text, "Abraham believed God, and it was reckoned as righteousness" (Rom 4:3). The passage is from Genesis 15:4–6—the earliest Yahweh source. I'll use the word "Yahweh" for God, which is the practice of this source. This passage says that Yahweh "brought him outside" and showed him the stars. Yahweh then asked him if he could number them. The answer was in effect apparently not. Yahweh then says, "So shall your descendants be." The passage then says, "And he believed Yahweh; and he reckoned it to him as righteousness" (Gen 15:5–6). What was the "it"? It is his believing Yahweh. The act of believing was reckoned to him as righteousness. The New English Bible translates this passage this way: "Abram put his faith in the Lord, and the Lord counted that faith to him as righteousness." It was not that the belief that he expressed was righteous, but Yahweh "reckoned it to him as righteousness."

Note that the passage in Genesis refers to Abram. Abram became Abraham, but this is the early Abram. The event involved Abram believing

Yahweh and what Yahweh said—a proposition. The passage also describes a metaphysical act—Yahweh reckoned him righteous. There are two things to note about this passage. There is no suggestion that Abraham was reckoned righteous once and for all—as some regard faith in the Christian tradition. The passage also does not say that Abram "believed in God" and then was reckoned righteous.

Believing in God is often thought to be one of the most important things one can do. One must put this passage in its context. Abram/Abraham became the main character in Genesis for about fourteen chapters beginning with chapter 12. Paul referred to him as "our forefather according to the flesh" (Rom 4:1). Important to the story is that Abram believed what Yahweh said. Yahweh said that his descendants will be as innumerable as the stars. The story goes on to say that the descendants of Abram will be slaves for four hundred years. They will then be given what is now referred to as "the promised land." It is bounded by the great river of Egypt and the Euphrates, and included the land of ten tribes. What Paul is doing is to tell the believers in Rome to identify with the God who calls for a jihad, a holy war, a war to slaughter people in city after city, after the Israelites crossed the Jordan. This God is also described as killing Egyptians in order for the Israelites to have something to brag about. It was not the prophets that impressed Paul but the Yahwist—the earliest source who introduced the exodus story and endorsed the invasion and slaughter in Palestine.

After saying that Abraham believed God and his belief was reckoned as righteousness, Paul applies this story to his readers. He says that it was not just Abraham who was to be reckoned as righteous. He says, "But the words 'reckoned to him as righteousness,' were written not for his sake alone, but for ours also" (Rom 4:23). Who is he referring to? He says, "[Those] who believe in him that raised from the dead Jesus our Lord, who was put to death for our trespasses and raised for our justification" (Rom 4:24–25). It seems to this author that Paul is giving an odd interpretation of what Yahweh is purported to have said. Yahweh is described as intending to say that not just Abraham was reckoned righteous, but also that "we believers" will be reckoned righteous. That's a significant leap. Maybe a Kierkegaardian leap of faith.

When it says that Abraham believed Yahweh, can the word "trust" be used here? Even though what Abraham believed was a proposition, one could properly argue that he believed this proposition because he trusted Yahweh. This, in effect, is Paul's argument in the last part of chapter 4.

## Part 2 — A Defense

When Abraham considered his age and the bareness of Sarah, Paul said of Abraham, "No distrust made him waver concerning the promise of God, but he grew strong in his faith as he gave glory to God" (Rom 4:20). The opposite of faith is distrust. Faith, here, is thus trust, not disbelief.

Borg refers to the words salvation, redemption and justification; he says of them that their meaning is linked to a transformation of life. Being reckoned righteous, however, does not refer to a transformation of life. Paul goes on to say that what applied to Abraham applies to the believer today.

Paul also has a view of the cross that undermines Borg's view. He says, "We are now justified by his blood" (Rom 5:9). Paul also says, "They [the believers] are justified by his grace as a gift, through the redemption which is in Christ Jesus, whom God put forward as an expiation by his blood to be received by faith" (Rom 3:24–25). Justification is de jure. It is not linked to a transformation of life.

What about the meanings of the words "salvation" and "redemption"? In chapter 8 Paul says that God has done something that the law could not do. "[By] sending his own Son . . . in order that the just requirement of the law might be fulfilled in us, who walk . . . according to the Spirit" (Rom 8:3–4). To say that the requirements of the law would be fulfilled in us is to say that our lives would be transformed. Borg seems right here. Later in chapter 12 he tells the Roman Christians, "Do not be conformed to this world be but be transformed by the renewal of your mind that ye may prove what is the what is the will of God, the good and acceptable and perfect" (Rom 12:2). If the actions of the Roman Christians can reflect what is good and perfect, then clearly their lives can be transformed and significantly changed.

The question then becomes how, for Paul, are our lives transformed? One possibility is that it is linked to what Paul says when he says, "The righteousness of God has been manifested apart from law" (Rom 3:21). He goes on to speak of "the righteousness of God through faith in Jesus Christ" (Rom 3:22). This righteousness could be understood in judicial terms. Salvation is then not a transformation of life, but judicial, finding forgiveness of sin. I think that this is the usual interpretation. However, to say that the righteousness of God has been manifest could mean that the righteous-making quality of God has been made manifest. How is this quality accessed? Paul says "through faith in Jesus Christ." The suggestion would be that for Paul the life of faith is a way of accessing God's righteousness. Through faith people are made righteous, not just de jure.

Paul also says this: "He who through faith is righteous shall live" (Rom 1:17). Believing something is not normally considered the basis for finding life.

Borg's view would also be consistent with his earlier statement about the gospel: "It is the power of God for salvation to everyone who has faith" (Rom 1:16). If power is involved, then something other than just forgiveness would seem to be involved—something such as the transformation of life. Salvation would then involve an on-going process of being transformed by a commitment to Christ, by faith.

In Romans 6:17 Paul refers to the believers in Rome as being "slaves of righteousness." He also refers to righteousness as a quality of God's kingdom (Rom 14:17). A commitment to Christ would thus also involve a commitment to righteousness.

Righteousness would then have to be distinguished from justification. Paul says, however, "They [individuals] are justified by his grace as a gift, through the redemption which is in Christ, whom God put forward as an expiation by his blood, to be received by faith" (Rom 3:24). He also says, "We are now justified by his blood" (Rom 5:8). If justification is a gift based on the cross, then justification is not linked to a transformation of lives in the sense that they are made better. A person might feel thankful and feel good about it, but the life would not necessarily be made better.

There are two questions at this point. Are these two things compatible? Is it consistent with what Paul says elsewhere?

A person can be justified and at the same time be in a process of being transformed. He tells his readers in Rome that they are to "yield your members to righteousness for sanctification" (Rom 6:19). Transformation would involve a commitment to Christ, which involves faith, a commitment to righteousness, and living according to the Spirit.

What about consistency with other things Paul has said? Consider Romans 10:9: "If you confess with your lips that Jesus is Lord and believe in your heart that God raised him from the dead, you will be saved." That wouldn't mean that your life would be transformed. It sounds like being saved from hell. This is analogous to what Paul says in discussing Abraham (Rom 4:22). Instead of saying you will be saved he says that you will be reckoned as righteous, which refers to justification. If there is no significant difference between salvation and justification, then Marcos Borg is wrong in thinking that salvation involves a transformation of life. If we look outside of Romans we find the following: "For by grace you have been saved through faith; and this is not your own doing, it is the gift of God" (Eph 2:8). If salvation is a gift, then it would not involve a transformation of life.

Scholars do not think, however, that all of the books attributed to Paul were written by Paul. Ephesians is one of those books that most scholars do not think was written by Paul.[3]

What's the conclusion? There are good reasons to believe that Borg is right, but also some reason to think that he is wrong. Maybe Paul was confused on this issue.

## THE ELEMENTS OF RELIGION

The first element of religion is values. In the prophets it wasn't difficult to determine their values because it belonged to their proclamations. In Paul one has to read very closely to figure out what his values are. His focus is more on spiritual hypotheticals, which is element two. Let's consider them.

### Elements Two and Six

His discussion of salvation involves three levels of concepts. First level: Here there is the discussion of the importance of faith, which he opposes to law and works. If Borg's interpretation is proper, then we have this spiritual hypothetical: if faith, then the transformation of life and righteousness is found. This would be life at its best. If he is wrong, then faith brings justification and a reservation in heaven—which he says brings life.

Here are some relevant passages: "The law brings wrath" (Rom 4:15). "When the law came I died," Paul said. "He who through faith is righteous shall live" (Rom 1:17).

Second level: The finding of life is through the Spirit. To live according to the flesh leads to human degradation. If we live according to the Spirit, then true life will be found. Relevant passages: "To set the mind on the flesh is death, but to set the mind on the Spirit is life and peace" (Rom 8:6). In other words, redemption would not be just about getting into heaven, but a transformed life linked to the Spirit.

Third level: Salvation is a matter of God's election. The discussion of election is in the last half of chapter 8 and chapter 9. If justification is a

---

3. Ibid., 351.

matter of faith, then a person may think of faith as something we do analogous to work. Paul cuts that off by introducing the notion of election.

Election is here described as part of God's purpose. He introduces this by means of a story in Genesis when Rebekah had two children in her womb and God said that the older shall serve the younger. This is not understood as a prediction but God's choice. Paul then has God say, "Jacob I loved but Esau I hated" (Rom 9:13). He then has God go on to say, "I will have mercy on whom I have mercy, and I will have compassion on whom I have compassion" (9:13). He then has God say, "He has mercy upon whomever he will, and he hardens the heart of whomever he wills" (9:18). The emphasis here is on God's freedom to choose.

Here we can see the roots of a conservative view of the divine command theory. God is free to command whatever he chooses to command. This view of the divine command theory we found in the Yahwist, the earliest of the Torah sources. It was also the source of the Abraham story in Genesis 15. It is also rooted in the theology of Barth. Paul seems to rely primarily on the Yahwist source.

Note that doctrine of election seems to undermine the spiritual hypotheticals that are found in earlier part of Romans, at levels one and two. A spiritual hypothetical is of the form "if one does X, then Y will happen." The assumption is that one can do X; otherwise it would make no sense. Deuteronomy has God say that if you keep the law, you will find life. Paul found that he could not keep the law. He thus dropped that spiritual hypothetical for his version of the gospel.

According to the doctrine of election, the first part of the spiritual hypothetical is determined by God's election. God is portrayed as having freedom to have us do X or not do X. That seems to rule out our freedom to be able to do X or not X, whatever X happens to be. Some philosophers and theologians may take issue with that. It seems to this writer, however, that the freedom to choose something and being elected to do that thing are incompatible.

Apart from the issue of freedom, some people will have moral grounds for rejecting his claim that "he [God] has mercy upon whomever he will, and he hardens the heart of whomever he wills" (Rom 9:18). Such a person may find solace in Romans 11:25–32. Here he is discussing the Gentiles and the sons of Israel. He says at one point that all Israel will be saved (Rom 11:25). He then regards the "consignment" of people to disobedience as a reason to show mercy. He says, "God has consigned all men to disobedience, that he may have mercy upon all" (Rom 11:32). This seems to refer to the universal salvation of everyone. It is as if sin is not intrinsically bad, but instead a reason for God to show mercy. If what is considered sin is a matter of God's free choice, then it would not be intrinsically bad.

With respect to the elements of religion, we found four spiritual hypotheticals at levels one and two: (1) If there is faith, then life can be found. (2) If works and law, then there is human degradation. (3) If we live according to the flesh, human degradation will be found. (4) If we live according to the Spirit, then true life will be found.

What Paul also says, which is not mentioned here, is that people are justified by faith—if faith then justification. That is not a spiritual hypothetical, however. In a spiritual hypothetical what follows the "if" and the "then" are experiences. That God justifies a person is not an experience, but a metaphysical statement.

Could justification mean transforming people, making them just? The problem here is that Paul also says, "We are now justified by his blood" (Rom 5:9). Justification seems to be judicial for Paul, de jure.

The interpretation of the first hypothetical is open to debate depending on how salvation is understood. If salvation involves a transformation of life, then the hypothetical could read: "if faith, then a transformation of life and a finding of life."

## Element One

We are now in a position to understand element one. This refers to values. For Paul the greatest value was God's act of sending his Son into the world "that the just requirements of the law might be fulfilled in us" (Rom 8:4).

The word "value," however, normally refers to qualities that a person can embrace. Regarded this way, the primary values seem to be faith and righteousness. Faith is a religious value; righteousness a moral value. Faith involves more than belief. It involves trust and sometimes a commitment.

Paul's emphasis on Genesis chapter 15 makes clear that he considers righteousness to be important. In Romans chapter 14 Paul says that for him the kingdom of God is righteousness, peace, and joy in the Holy Spirit. In chapter 7 Paul says to his believers in Rome that they were once slaves of sin and "have become slaves of righteousness" (Rom 6:17). He then refers to himself as speaking in human terms, and then says to them, "Yield your members to righteousness for sanctification" (Rom 6:19).

Faith might be understood as a way of accessing God's righteous making qualities. They would then be closely tied together. Peace and joy supplement these values. In the introduction to each letter Paul normally says, "Grace to you and peace from God our Father and the Lord Jesus Christ."

## Element Three

In understanding his theology his view of human nature is important. The common view is that for Paul nothing we can do has any value. One has to look carefully, however, at what he says in particular contexts. When he tells his readers to yield their members to righteousness, he is assuming that this is something that they can do. If salvation is a transformation of people's lives, then it is possible that righteousness can be achieved "through faith in Jesus Christ" (Rom 3:22). On the other hand, this righteousness could be "reckoned righteousness" as was the case with Abraham and linked to the cross.

Paul's description of his own nature supports the view that we can do nothing that has any value. He says,

> I am carnal, sold under sin. I do not understand my own actions. For I do not do what I want, but I do the very thing I hate. Now if I do what I do not want, I agree that the law is good. So then it no longer I that do it, but sin which dwells with me. For I know that nothing good dwells within me, that is, in my flesh (Rom 7:14–18).

The surprising thing here is that he does not consider himself responsible for his actions, but sin that is within him. This does not support the view that righteousness is something that can be achieved except for a de jure type of righteous as with Abraham and through the cross.

Supplementing his view of human nature is his view of what happens when law and human decision making come together. What happens is that a collision occurs with disastrous results. When the law came, I died, said Paul. "The very commandment which promised life proved to be death to me" (Rom 7:10). In keeping with that, Paul takes a passage about law in Deuteronomy and applies it to his preaching of the gospel. Deuteronomy 30:11–14 says that the law conforms to human nature and is the source of life—a spiritual hypothetical. Paul takes this passage and applies it to the gospel he preaches. Where this passage speaks of the law, Paul inserts "the word of faith we preach" (Rom 10:6–8). He turns what Deuteronomy has to say on its head.

This illustrates how element three—beliefs about human nature—are important to spiritual hypotheticals. A shift in interpretation of element three causes a shift in interpretation of element two. Note also how interpretations of element three are empirical, rooted in human experience and observations. It is not obtuse material, for which we need a special revelation. It is material we learn in observing people, interacting with people, and studying history.

How do we understand the statement that the law brings spiritual death or wrath (Rom 4:14)? As a Pharisee he knew that the first psalm considered law as a source of well-being and knew that Deuteronomy claims this. Why is he objecting to Scripture? The only explanation, it seems to me, lies in his religious experience. "When the commandment came sin revived and I died," he said (Rom 7:10). Chapter 7 uses "I," "me," or "myself" about forty times.

Martin Luther's experience was like Paul's experience. Someone told Luther that he took religion too seriously. Both were perfectionist whose perfectionism led to spiritual death.

In chapter 12 we will examine O. Hobart Mower's critique of Paul's view of the gospel.

## PAUL'S PORTRAIT IN ACTS

The question now is how Romans compares to the portrait of Paul in Acts—a book which may have been written fifty years later.

Acts 13:38–39 has Paul saying that forgiveness of sins is proclaimed through Jesus; and "by him every one that believes is freed from everything from which you could not be freed by the law of Moses." Here we have Paul's contrast between law and gospel with an emphasis on belief. Note that "being freed" is a metaphysical thing, not something linked to people's experiences.

After a sermon of Paul, we find the following: "As many as were ordained to eternal life believed" (13:48). This fits his doctrine of election and his emphasis on belief. In chapter 16 Paul and Silas are asked the question of what must be done to be saved. Answer: "Believe in the Lord Jesus and you will be saved, you and your household" (16:31).

"Believe in" could refer to trust since a person is involved not a proposition. The oddity is to apply it to the household. If "saved" meant a transformation of life, it is hard to see how the transformation of one's life would assure the transformation of the life of the rest of the household.

Maybe this is Luke's view of Paul, and not Paul. Note: I am using the name "Luke" to refer to the author of Luke-Acts. We do not know, however, who wrote the book entitled the Gospel according to Luke. The name was added later.

There is one other speech attributed to Paul given at the Areopagus, in chapter 17. This speech is significantly different. Here Paul is described as saying of God, "He is not far from each of us, for 'in him we live and move and have our being'; even as some of your poets have said, 'For indeed we are his offspring'" (17:27–28). It is the Stoics who believed that God was the soul of the universe in whom we live and have our being. God and universe are not separate entities.

"Not far from us" is like the author of Deuteronomy who says of Israel that it has a god that is near to them (4:7). To this he adds that he has a commandment that is not hard or far off (30:11). This is clearly not like the message we find in Romans.

## PETER'S PORTRAIT IN ACTS

The next question is this: Are the views in the first twelve chapters of Acts similar to what is found in Romans and in the last part of Acts? Whereas Paul plays the major role in the latter part of Acts, Peter plays that role in the first twelve chapters.

In four speeches Peter emphasizes the importance of repentance. At his sermon at Pentecost he concludes by saying, "Repent and be baptized every one of you" (2:38). This is also found in Acts 3:18, 5:29–32, and 11:18. Note that in our outline of Paul's view of the gospel in Romans, no mention of repentance was found. Salvation is by grace through faith, which is a gift and a matter of God's election. Salvation for Paul is a matter of God's actions. Repentance, however, is something we do.

It could be argued that for Paul to have faith presupposes that one has repented. Paul refers to Abraham, however, as a prime example of a man of faith. "Abraham believed God and it was reckoned to him as righteousness" (Rom 4:3). There is no concept of repentance in the Abraham story. Thus faith does not presuppose repentance.

## Part 2—A Defense

Paul does mention repentance in the second chapter of Romans. He says, "For he [God] will render to every man according to his works" (2:7). In this context he says, "Do you not know that God's kindness is meant to lead you to repentance" (2:4). From this, one would expect that Paul would say that there are those who will be moved by God's kindness, repent, and find salvation. In the rest of Romans, however, he rejects this; he never mentions repentance. In the next chapter he says, "All men, both Jews and Greeks, are under the power of sin, as it is written, 'none is righteous, no, not one'" (3:9–10). "For no human being will be justified in his sight by works of the law." What about God's kindness and repentance mentioned in chapter 2? Cannot repentance lead to forgiveness? The odd thing is that they end up playing no role in Paul's view of the gospel.

It is possible that for Paul the power of sin makes repentance impossible. Many interpreters of Paul would say that we are so corrupt that we cannot do anything good that would help our salvation. Repentance would be doing something to help our salvation.

Another incompatibility between Paul's and Acts' views of Jesus is found in Peter's second speech. Referring to Jesus he speaks of him as one who God had spoken about in the prophets. Referring to Deuteronomy 18:15, he says, "Moses said, 'The Lord God will raise up for you a prophet from your brethren as he raised me up. You shall listen to him'" (Acts 3:22). In other words, Jesus is portrayed as a second Moses. This is a theme emphasized in Matthew's gospel. If Jesus was a second Moses, should not the Christian life be based on the law he proclaimed? If Jesus restated the law, why should faith be an alternative to law? Matthew says that he who tones down the least of "these commandments" shall be called least in the kingdom of heaven (Matt 5:19).

As mentioned before, on this issue there is a significant theological divide. The question seems to be over whether Christian faith should be considered a religion about Jesus, as Paul portrays it; or whether Christian faith should be considered as the religion of Jesus. The latter we find in the Synoptic Gospels.

Besides this emphasis on law, we find after Peter's first sermon on Pentecost the following: "And all who believed were together and had all things in common; and they sold their possessions and goods and distributed them to, as any had need" (Acts 2:44). Later, in Acts 4:32 after another sermon, this same thing happens again. The author seems to assume that his audience was familiar with the preaching of Jesus and from that understood that coming together and sharing everything in common was the appropriate thing to do. There is nothing in Acts, however, that provides that background information. This tells us at least something of Luke's view of the message of Jesus. He may have understood that sharing what one has with others may have been implied by the command to love one's neighbor as oneself.

If we look at the first twelve chapters of Acts through the lens of the elements of religion, what do we find? When law is emphasized, then values will be emphasized, but no particular values are mentioned. The one exception is the ideal of a community coming together and sharing everything in common. If law is important, however, then the assumption is going to be that the law conforms to human nature. It is pointless to emphasize law if law and human nature are seen as a fatal crash bringing death. When law is emphasized repentance is likely to be emphasized. This is mentioned four times in sermons attributed to Peter.

The book of Acts is probably in part an idealized portrait of the early Christian movement, but not entirely. The distinction between what the author of Acts has Peter say and what he has Paul say is significant. It is clear that Luke is not just reading his own views into the substance of the book. Besides, most of what he has Paul say reflects what Paul said in his letters. What is found in the early chapters of Acts could thus reflect a tradition that predates Paul.

What would be the source of such material? Howard Clark Kee mentions that Papias of Hierapolis, a second-century bishop, said that Mark is said to have remembered sayings of Jesus from conversations with Peter.[4] This would be relevant since Luke-Acts uses Mark. He also mentions that Justin Martyr (CE 100?–165?) refers to Mark's gospel as a memoir from Peter.[5] He bases this on something that Papias said. The implication is that Mark could have had sources that predate Paul. Since the author of Luke-Acts makes use of Mark, Peter's portrait could be tied to a tradition that predates Paul.

## SUMMARY

We began our discussion of Romans by noting how Paul's view of the gospel is controversial. It is often believed that faith is belief, and salvation is

---

4. Kee, *Jesus in History*, 136.
5. Ibid., 137.

finding forgiveness of sin and a reservation in heaven. Borg argues that faith is loyalty or trust, and salvation is a transformation of life. In a couple of passages we saw that faith seems to be commitment, even a passionate commitment. In the discussion of Abraham, faith involved believing what Yahweh said, but that seemed to involve trusting Yahweh. Paul then applies the same logic to the contemporary believer, where the belief is that God raised Jesus from the dead. Faith then seemed to involve trusting God.

Borg is also concerned about how redemption, salvation, and justification are often understood. Paul says that God sent Christ into the world to fulfill in people the demands of the law. That would involve transforming human lives, not just an atonement on the cross. The question then arises as to how this is supposed to be achieved. A possibility was suggested. Paul says that righteousness of God has been manifest apart from the law (Rom 3:21). The suggestion was made that this might have meant that the righteous-making quality of God has been made manifest. Paul goes on to say that the righteous of God comes through faith in Jesus Christ. Faith would then be a means of accessing this righteous-making quality and finding righteousness. Life is then transformed.

Borg's point of view has two problems. Borg says that salvation, reconciliation, and justification involve a transformation of life. For Paul, however, justification comes as a gift through faith by means of the cross. "We are now justified by his blood," Paul said (Rom 4:7). What comes by way of the blood would not be transformation.

The second problem is that sometimes Paul does not seem to recognize a significant different between salvation and justification.

In applying the elements of religion to what Paul says in Romans, we found four spiritual hypotheticals, two values, and a view of human nature. The four spiritual hypotheticals spiritual hypotheticals: if faith, then salvation; if works and law, then spiritual death; if life according to the Spirit, then life and peace; if life according to the flesh, then spiritual death is found. The primary values were faith and righteousness. The view of human nature is that the law and human nature collide, but the gospel is compatible with human nature and a source of life.

After emphasizing these spiritual hypotheticals and values, Paul introduced the concept of election. He says that God will have mercy on whomever he wills, and he hardens the heart of whomever he wills (Rom 9:18). The emphasis is on God's freedom, and it assumes what was called earlier a conservative view of the divine command theory.

Is that consistent with the values and the spiritual hypotheticals emphasized earlier? This author does not think so.

We saw in Acts, which was written at least thirty years later, the same basic theology attributed to Paul that is found in Romans. The exception to this is the very last sermon which conflicts with Paul's basic theology. Here his view of human nature is akin to what is found in Deuteronomy as opposed to Romans. The claim in that sermon is that God is not far from us. Deuteronomy said that they had a God who was akin to them. He went on to say that their God was wise and his law was the source of life and well-being—just the opposite of what Paul said.

We found a significantly different theology in the first part of Acts where Peter is the dominating figure. There we found an emphasis on repentance and law. Jesus is portrayed as a second Moses, much like we find in Matthew's gospel. We do not find particular laws, but we find the ideal of the church sharing all of their goods in common. This could have been an interpretation of the command to love your neighbor as yourself.

# 9

# Early Christianity
## The Synoptic Gospels

WE HAVE EXAMINED THE logic of Paul's classic statement of the gospel in Romans. We have seen that this basically agrees with how the author of Luke portrays the views of Paul in the last part of Acts. The basic ideas are that the law plus works yields human degradation, spiritual death. Salvation is by grace through faith and through God's election. To live by the Spirit is to find life. We then saw that this differs from the portrait of Peter's views found in the first part of Acts. There the emphasis was upon repentance and the law. In this section we are going to focus on the Synoptic Gospels. John's gospel will be covered to a great extent in chapter 10, which is on Christology.

The question now is this: How do the elements of religion shed light on the Synoptics and how do they compare with the views of Paul?

The phrase "Synoptic Gospels" refer to the first three gospels in the New Testament—Matthew, Mark, and Luke. "Optic" expresses the idea of view. "Syn" expresses the idea of being together or with. The word "synoptic" thus implies that they have a common view.

To understand them it helps to take into consideration how they relate to one another. In the nineteenth century it was commonly thought that Mark was an abbreviation of Matthew. Since then, however, scholars have coalesced around the concept that Mark is the earliest gospel and Matthew and Luke make use of Mark. Ninety percent of Mark is found in Matthew and about sixty percent in Luke. Sometimes the precise words used by Mark are found in the other two gospels. Sometimes one will abbreviate and use fewer words than what Mark uses. Sometimes Matthew or Luke will clean up Mark's language which is not very good. Sometimes Mark and Matthew will agree and Luke will be different. Sometimes Mark and Luke will agree and Matthew different. However, one does not find Matthew and Luke agreeing and Mark different. Mark is the common denominator upon which the other two build.

Matthew and Luke have material in common; sometimes word for word, not found in Mark. This has convinced scholars that we have a different source. This is referred to as Q from the German "quela," meaning source. That gives us four types of material. Mark, Q, what is uniquely Matthew, and what is uniquely Luke. This allows us to see how Matthew and Luke adjust the material in Mark based on their style of writing and interests.

Protestants usually equate the gospel with Paul's statement of the gospel, but the New Testament begins with four books that have in their title "gospel." These titles were not given by the authors. Nevertheless, they tell us how the early church perceived these books. Mark's gospel has this opening line: "The beginning of the gospel of Jesus Christ, the son of God." This is a reference to the book itself. It appears that "the gospel of Jesus Christ" might have been the title of the book. The problem is that we have two similar books attributed to Matthew and Luke. John's gospel differs significantly, but it is also a statement of the gospel. We thus have four statements of the gospel, each using the phrase "according to."

From the perspective of the doctrine of the inerrancy of Scripture, something odd is going on here. According to Thomas Aquinas all Scripture is supposed to be according to God and based on divine knowledge. However, with the writings of Paul, we end up with at least five interpretations of the gospel.

In the mid 1980s a project was started by the Society of Biblical Literature to produce a documented reconstruction of Q. The initial English version was finished in 2000. In his book *Q, the Earliest Gospel*, John S. Kloppenborg argues that Q is properly understood as the earliest statement of the gospel. If he is right that would give us at least six interpretations of the gospel—Paul, John, Matthew, Mark, Luke, and Q.

The Greek word translated "gospel" is *euangelion*. It was used by Paul to apply to the message that spelled out the implications that the death and

## Part 2 — A Defense

resurrection of Jesus had for human beings. Howard Clark Kee notes that it was also used to denote the benefits that the empire enjoyed because of the authority of Caesar, the divinely appointed emperor.[1] Caesar was recognized as a miracle worker and a healer, one that can redeem people from their difficulties. The benefits that accrue to Roman citizens are because of a divinely appointed emperor. What Christians did, he says, was to take that theology and apply it to Jesus. They claimed that Jesus was the divine appointed one. There is thus reason to believe that these books are called gospel because they proclaim the benefits which come through Jesus, the divinely appointed one. The titles would thus seem to imply a spiritual hypothetical.

### ELEMENT ONE: VALUES

The first element of religion refers to beliefs and assumptions about values. In Mark the baptism of Jesus is very important because it introduces the reader to Jesus. Unlike Matthew and Luke, it has no birth story. At his baptism Jesus hears a voice say, "Thou art my Son." This is followed by the statement "with thee I am well pleased" (Mark 1:12). The odd thing about this translation is that the verb used here for "I am well pleased" is in the aorist tense. This tense is used of events or actions that have taken place in the past. The suffix of the verb is "eu" which refers to something good. "Am well pleased" is not an event. It does not refer to anything in the past. The passage is thus saying that God did something in the past with respect to Jesus that was for the good. The best translation of this seems to be the statement "with thee I have willed the good." As an introduction to the ministry of Jesus, this would imply that his future ministry would be the embodiment of what is good, an embodiment of the highest values.

It would be beyond the scope of this chapter to track down all of the values mentioned in the various Synoptics. The major emphases, however, are (1) the law in general, (2) the two greatest commandments, (3) the importance of social justice, and (4) a statement of the ideal of being servants of one another. They also focused on the importance of the kingdom of God, but we are going to put off that discussion until later.

The law and the prophets permeated the world and culture in which Jesus lived. Mark, the shortest and earliest gospel, begins by quoting the prophet Isaiah. He then has eight discussions of the law in its sixteen

---

1. Kee, *Jesus in History*, 133.

chapters. Jesus criticizes his critics for focusing on tradition as opposed to the commands of God (7:5). He has two discussions on the Sabbath (2:27; 3:4), a discussion of divorce (10:2), on taxes to be paid to Caesar (12:16), on food laws (7:20), and then a statement of the greatest commandments—to love God with all one's heart and to love one's neighbor as oneself (12:28-31).

Note that the love commandment embodies two principles. The command to love (*agape*) is a command to act for the well-being of others. The "as oneself" recognizes the appropriateness of self-love and implies equality. Each person is of equal value.

Immediately after stating that a person should love his neighbor as himself Luke introduces a discussion of who a neighbor is (Luke 10:25-28). He then tells the story of the Good Samaritan. Since the Samaritans were religious outcasts, the idea of a Good Samaritan was an anomaly. Luke is thus clarifying whose one's neighbor is, and indicating that the principle of social justice is implied by the commandment to love one's neighbor.

Mark introduces the social justice theme early in his book by having the critics of Jesus criticizing him for eating with tax collectors and "sinners" (2:16-17). Both Matthew (11:19) and Luke (15:12) pick up this same material. The word "sinners" here refers to a group of people with whom one is not supposed to socialize because they were not considered keepers of the law. The first psalm says that one should not stand with sinners nor sit with scoffers.

The ideal of being servants of one another is introduced in Mark to draw a contrast between the nature of his kingdom and the practices of the Gentiles. It says that the Gentiles who have authority lord it over their subjects. In his kingdom, however, "whoever would be the first among you must be your servant" (Mark 10:41). Luke 22:25-27 and Matthew 20:26-27 also pick up this theme. Note that Gentiles are regarded as "those guys" and looked down upon. Mark is fairly early. Later in John it is the Jews who are "those guys."

## ELEMENT TWO: SPIRITUAL HYPOTHETICALS

The second element of religion refers to beliefs and assumptions about spiritual hypotheticals. Since "gospel" means good news, something good for human well-being, the word itself would seem to imply a spiritual hypothetical. It was mentioned above that this is the view of Howard Clark

Kee. Earlier we found such spiritual hypotheticals in Amos, Jeremiah, and Isaiah. The prophets addressed society and they perceived God as embodying justice and righteousness. They then perceived that in seeking the Lord the society would find life. "Seek the Lord and live," said Amos. The gospels introduce a different emphasis because Jesus is portrayed as interacting sometimes with just one person and often with a group of individuals. The practice of healing reflects this.

The authors of the Synoptics, however, were in the tradition of the law and the prophets by perceiving life to be found in the law. Matthew 19:17 has Jesus say, "If you would enter life, keep the commandments." In Luke, Jesus is described as saying that the person who keeps the primary commandments will find life (Luke 10:28). Mark says that the person who hears and accepts the preaching of the kingdom will "bear fruit, thirtyfold and sixtyfold and a hundredfold" (Mark 4:20).

Mark 8:35 says, "For whoever would save his life will lose it; and whoever loses his for my sake and the gospel's will save it." Here we have a spiritual hypothetical which is picked up both by Matthew (10:39) and Luke (17:13). Here there is a play on the words "lose" and "save." To save one's life in the bad sense is to look after one's short-term interests. "Lose" in the bad sense is not to lose it physically, but to have one's life disintegrate and not achieve its potential. To save life in the good sense is to find life at its very best. The message is this: Whoever seeks merely short-term self-interest will not really find life as it can and should be. On the other hand, the person who goes beyond short-term self-interest and is a disciple will find life as it can and should be.

## THE KINGDOM OF GOD

Mark has Jesus begin his ministry by saying, "The time is fulfilled, and the kingdom of God is at hand; repent, and belief in the gospel" (Mark 1:15). We find the same thing in Matthew 4:17. What is it to claim that the kingdom of God is at hand? There was a German liberal tradition which interpreted the kingdom of God as something spiritual which could be achieved—Albrecht Ritschl, Adolf Harnack. This is analogous to Paul's view that the kingdom is righteousness and peace and joy in the Holy Spirit (Rom 14:17).

As opposed to this spiritual view, we find in Mark 9:1 the following: "Truly I say to you, there are some standing here who will not taste death, before they see the kingdom of God come with power." The entire chapter 13 of Mark is devoted to what will happen in the future before the kingdom comes. It will involve rumors of wars, and then nations will rise up against nations. Earthquakes will occur and famines. "For in those days there will be there will be such tribulation as has not been from the beginning of the creation which God created until now" (Mark 13:19). Even more of this type of material is found in Matthew chapters 24 and 25.

The view is that the world will go down the drain. God will then intervene by way of judgment and then establish his kingdom on earth. This is referred to as apocalypticism and Jesus is referred to as an apocalyptic prophet.

The background of this is chapter 9 of Daniel which says that when the end comes there will be a flood and war. It then says, "Upon the wing of abominations shall come one who makes desolate, until the decreed end is poured out on the desolator" (Dan 9:27).

The notion that God will establish an ideal kingdom on earth goes back to the early prophets—Isaiah 2, Amos 8:13–15, Micah 4, Jeremiah 23:5–6. The book of Daniel comes much later and is considered one of the latest Hebrew Scriptures—second century BCE.[2] In its last chapter it speaks again of the end when "there shall be a time of trouble, such as never has been since there was a nation till that time" (Dan 12:1). It then speaks of a resurrection: "Many of those who sleep in the dust of the earth shall awake, some to everlasting life, and some to shame and everlasting contempt" (12:2).

A big issue in New Testament studies is the issue of whether Jesus should be considered an apocalyptic prophet. One of the most important and influential books in the twentieth century was Albert Schweitzer's book *The Quest of the Historical Jesus* (1906). He argues that Jesus was an apocalyptic prophet. His criticism of prior scholars is that they have missed seeing Jesus as a first-century Jew.

Despite Jesus' mistaken view of the future, Schweitzer was much impressed with his focus on the kingdom of God and with the influence his spirit has had upon the world. "For the main characteristic of Jesus," he says, "is that he looks beyond the consummation and salvation of the individual to a consummation and salvation of the world and to an elect mankind. He is completely filled with and determined by desire and hope

---

2. West, *Introduction to the Old Testament*, 469–84.

for the kingdom of God."³ This meant for Schweitzer a desire and hope for a moral consummation of all things. He also said, "Jesus means something to our world because a mighty spiritual force streams forth from him and flows through our time also. This fact can neither be shaken nor conformed by any historical discovery."⁴ In fact, he wishes to say, historical scholarship gets in the way. Individuals should be left alone with the sayings of Jesus.⁵

To understand Schweitzer it helps to put him in his historical context. In the nineteenth century it was common for scholars to belief that Matthew was the earliest gospel and Mark was a shortened version of Matthew. That was Schweitzer's perspective. Putting Matthew first makes a difference in understanding the historical Jesus.

Let's compare Matthew and Mark. Matthew is more conservative and has a greater emphasis on apocalypticism. He is more conservative in terms of his view of the law, and more conservative in terms of his vision of the ministry of Jesus. Both have Jesus begin his ministry by having him say: Repent, the kingdom of God is at hand (Mark 1:15; Matt 3:2). Matthew goes from there into the Sermon on the Mount, which is unique to him. There he considers the law to be stricter than the Mosaic Law. Moses said do not commit adultery. Matthew has Jesus say, "Everyone who looks at a woman lustfully has already committed adultery with her in his heart" (Matt 5:28). He then goes on to apply a stricter interpretation of divorce and swearing. He also goes beyond the law of loving one's neighbor as oneself. He says that one should love one's enemy (Matt 5:34).

How strict should the law be interpreted? Matthew says, "Whoever then relaxes one of the least of these commandments and teaches men so, shall be called least in the kingdom of heaven; but he who does them and teaches them shall be called great in the kingdom of heaven" (Matt 5:17–20). The spirit of Matthew is conveyed in his having Jesus say, "You, therefore, must be perfect, as your heavenly Father is perfect" (Matt 5:48).

Consider Mark's perspective of the law. Mark has two discussions of the Sabbath. In one case his disciples are criticized for not keeping the Sabbath. They were picking up grain when walking through a field of grain. Jesus says, "The Sabbath was made for man, not man for the Sabbath" (2:27). In other words, the law is for the sake of human beings and human well-being. Exceptions would then be appropriate when they maximize

---

3. Schweitzer, *Quest of the Historical Jesus*, 480.
4. Ibid., 479.
5. Ibid.

human well-being. In the other discussion, Jesus is criticized for healing on the Sabbath. His response, "Is it lawful on the Sabbath to do good or to do harm, to save life or to kill" (3:4). In other words, primacy is to be given to maximizing people's well-being. Law is a means to do this.

What we have here is a liberal view of law. Law is for the sake of human well-being. It should be understood and interpreted this way. This is consistent with regarding love of neighbor as being primary. If each law is important in and of itself and to relax one is to do wrong, then there is no path to follow when love conflicts with something else.

Mark 7:1–23 has scribes and Pharisees observe the disciples of Jesus eating without having properly washed their hands as the traditional interpretation of the law prescribes. Jesus responds by criticizing their critics. What is important, he says, is not what one puts into the stomach but rather what comes out of the heart. This is to say, that it is the passions and feelings that are important. "For from within, out of the heart of man, come evil thoughts, fornication, theft, murder, adultery, coveting, wickedness, deceit, licentiousness, envy, slander, pride, foolishness" (7:36).

Note that it is moral vices that come out of the heart. The point of the discussion is thus to emphasize the importance of the moral dimension of life. Mark then adds to this a parenthetical remark: "Thus he declared all foods to be clean" (Mark 7:25). Matthew picks up this passage, Matthew 15:15–20, but he leaves out this last statement. Earlier Matthew had said that the person who relaxes one of the least of the commandments and teaches others to do so would called be least in the kingdom (Matt 5:19). Here Mark is expunging a whole area of law from the books. Matthew starts by using Mark and then modifies it a bit to fit his interests and concerns. His concern here was about the nature of law. Excluding an entire area of law would be much worse that toning down one of the laws.

Matthew's more conservative view of law fits apocalypticism better than Mark's liberal view. If the world is perceived as going down the drain, then a stricter conservative interpretation of the law is likely to be embraced. This can be seen in the more conservative movements in Islam, Judaism, and Christianity. Consider Al Qaida in Islam, the ultra-orthodox in Judaism, and fundamentalism in Christianity. In each case the world is seen as going down the drain and in each case there exist stricter, more conservative views of what is proper. Mark's liberal interpretation of law is a significant contrast to this.

Matthew also has a more conservative view of the mission of Jesus. In both gospels Jesus is portrayed as sending his disciples out to preach and heal. In Matthew he says, "Go nowhere among the Gentiles, and enter no town of the Samaritans, but go rather to the lost sheep of the house of Israel" (Matt 10:5). There is nothing analogous to this in Mark. What a difference this makes in understanding the ministry of Jesus. What about Luke's Good Samaritan story? It makes sense that Matthew would leave it out. Amos portrays God as loving non-Israelite nations and as liberating not just the Israelites (Amos 9:7). Matthew takes a step backward.

When Jesus sent out his disciples to heal and preach, Matthew has Jesus have them preach, "The kingdom of God is at hand" (Matt 10:7). What does Mark say? "So they went out and preached that men should repent" (Mark 6:12). Matthew switched "repent" to "the kingdom of God is at hand."

In keeping with this greater emphasis on the kingdom of God, Matthew concludes his directions to his disciples by saying, "When they persecute you in one town, flee to the next: for truly, I say to you, you will not have gone through the towns of Israel, before the Son of man comes" (Matt 10:23). This is odd in that the disciples play an important role in the latter part of Matthew. Note that it is "the Son of man that comes." There is a question as to whom he is referring to. Mark does not link the kingdom to Jesus sending out his disciples.

Matthew has John the Baptist preach, "Repent, for the kingdom of God is at hand" (Matt 3:2). Mark has John preaching "baptism of repentance for the forgiveness of sins" (Mark 1:4). There is no mention of the kingdom. That's two places where Matthew replaces talk of repentance with talk of the kingdom of God. In addition Matthew adds a number of parables and other material on the kingdom not found in Mark. See, for example, Matthew 13:44–49 and material in chapters 24 and 25 of Matthew.

Matthew picks up Mark's story of Peter coming to recognize that Jesus as the Messiah, but adds a conservative twist to it. He has Jesus say to Peter, "You are Peter, and on this rock will I build my church, and the powers of death shall no prevail against it" (Matt 16:18). The concept that there will be a church that represents him and that it will be strong and prevail is clearly a conservative emphasis.

Early in his gospel, chapter 4, Mark has Jesus teaching three parables of the kingdom that are not apocalyptic. One of them compares the kingdom to a mustard seed, which it says is the smallest seed. It then says that this seed becomes the greatest of all bushes (Mark 4:26–32). The message is that the kingdom of God begins small and grows to be that which is the greatest of all things. There is no apocalypticism here. Rather than portray the world going down the drain, the emphasis in on progress and development. The other parables also liken the kingdom to seed that grows and develops. In one of the parables the planting of the seed is likened to a preaching of the word (Mark 4:15). What a difference this makes in one's attitude toward the future.

There are other passages that fit this view of the kingdom. In Luke the Pharisees are portrayed as asking Jesus when the kingdom of God was coming. His answer: "The kingdom of God is not coming with signs to be observed; nor will they say, 'Lo, here it is!' or 'There!' for behold the kingdom of God is in the midst of you" (Luke 17:21). The kingdom is thus present. Luke 11:20 says, "But if it is by the finger of God that I cast out demons, then the kingdom of God has come upon you." That says that the kingdom of God is partially present. Both are consistent with the parable of the mustard seed.

Many of Schweitzer's readers had been influenced by Heinrich Julius Holtzmann (1832–1910). Holtzmann had argued that Mark's gospel provided the basic framework for understanding the history of Jesus' ministry. In his *Quest of the Historical Jesus* Schweitzer argues effectively that Mark does not have a consistent story to tell of the history of Jesus' ministry. Given the different views of the kingdom found in Mark, maybe we should say the same thing about his theology. He may have just put together traditions he learned about without trying to work out a consistent theology. An alternative would be to say that Mark was aware of the conflict between the two traditions but did not know which one was the proper one. He thus gives us both of them.

One thing is clear—the Synoptic Gospels do not give us a consistent theology. There are conflicting views of the law, the kingdom, and the mission of Jesus. In discussing the Torah the point was made that Scripture gives us conflicting theologies. Since there is more than one interpretation of the elements, Scripture cannot determine the proper interpretation. Scripture provides the context where the games of theology are played, but it doesn't provide how to play the game. The elements of religion seek to provide the rules for how to play the game. The game is to work out the best interpretations of the elements of religion.

PART 2—A DEFENSE

Too much effort has been focused on the puzzle of the historical Jesus. Schweitzer says that he agrees with this. Nevertheless, he has a view of the historical Jesus which he calls thoroughgoing eschatology.

Note that it is theology that shapes people's lives and can shape a culture. It makes claims about what is truly important. History is an empirical study. Such a study cannot verify or falsify Harnack's theology or liberation theology. Harnack claims that the soul has "infinite value." That cannot be verified or falsified by appeal to the historical Jesus. Liberation theology has a view about the structure of society and the role of capitalism in shaping the character of society. Nothing about the history of Jesus can verify or falsify this.

## JOHN HICK AND APOCALYPTICISM

John Hick was mentioned in chapter 1. He is probably the most influential philosopher in the late twentieth century and early twenty-first century. He considers Jesus to be an apocalyptic prophet. He then uses that perspective to criticize liberation theology and similar perspectives. The belief in an imminent kingdom, he says, had practical consequences: "It meant that Jesus' moral teaching did not involve a critique of the social, political and economic structures of his time in the manner of some of the earlier Hebrew prophets and of contemporary liberation theology."[6]

This sounds like Adolf von Harnack. Harnack said that it was the individual, not the state, that was to be redeemed.[7] Unlike Hick, however, he did not have an apocalyptic perspective. For him the kingdom of God was a spiritual force within you.[8] In chapter 15 we will see that Rauschenbusch was critical of the conservative social views of the liberal German theologians. What they failed to see, he said, is that the society itself needed to be redeemed. His claim was that what was present in the early prophets, such as Amos, was also present in the message and work of Jesus.

What is it to critique a social structure of a society? Let us suppose that there is a belief in a society that certain types of individuals ought to be treated in a special way. Let also suppose there is a practice based on this belief. Do we not then have a social structure? Traditional societies have had special norms for treating women, children, and gay persons. Modern

6. Hick, *Metaphor of Incarnation*, 21.
7. Harnack, *What Is Christianity?*, 60.
8. Ibid., 61.

white societies have had special norms for treating blacks. These norms have shaped the structures of many societies.

What about the society in which Jesus lived? At times we may have to dig beneath the surface to determine what the norms were. At times they are on the surface. The criticism of Jesus for eating with tax collectors and sinners (Mark 2:16) is obviously a criticism of him for breaking a norm. This type of point is made a half-dozen times in the various Synoptics. For example: "The Son of man came eating and drinking, and they say, 'Behold, a glutton and a drunkard, a friend of tax collectors and sinners'" (Matt 11:19). It would be arbitrary to avoid all of that material.

A parable in which a social outcaste ends up being the hero of the story is clearly a criticism of the social structure of the society. This is the case with the Good Samaritan story.

There is a rationale behind these stories—carrying out the implications of loving one's neighbor as oneself. This would include the sinner, tax collector, and the Samaritan.

If we dig beneath the surface, there is treasure to be found. To understand any society it is important to understand its attitudes toward women and children. In the first century, women and children lacked the standing and importance they are assumed to have in modern liberal societies. They were looked down upon as inferior kinds of beings.[9] Examining the gospels through this lens can yield significant results. Consider Mark 10:14: "Let the children come to me, do not hinder them; for to such belongs the kingdom of God."

Mark 10:29–31: "Many who are first will be last and the last will be first." Luke referring to this kingdom says, "And behold, some are last who will be first, and some who are first will be last" (Luke 13:30). What would be a modern translation of this point? A suggestion: "Many who are in the upper one per cent will be at the bottom and many at the bottom will be at the top." That is clearly a critique of the social structure of the society.

How much of this material is tied to the historical Jesus? The answer to that question I do not think that we can know with certainty. Nevertheless, there is much of this material embedded in the Synoptic Gospels. It is improper to choose which verses are historical based on one's theology. If Hick thinks that his theology is better than liberation theology, then he should defend it on the basis of theology, not on what he thinks is historical.

---

9. For an expanded discussion of this, see Ehrman, *Jesus: Apocalyptic Prophet*, 187–90.

## ELEMENT THREE: HUMAN NATURE

What about human nature, the third element? If keeping the greatest commandments is a source of life (Luke 10:28), then human nature must be compatible with keeping those commandments. If a person who accepts the preaching of the kingdom bears fruit (Mark 4:20), then there must be a compatibility between the kingdom and human nature. This is in the tradition of Deuteronomy, which saw compatibility between human nature and the law and saw the law as the source of life and what is good.

This contrasts with the view of Paul. For him the law did not conform to human nature. It brought spiritual death. "When the commandment came, sin revived and I died" (Rom 7:9).

The phrase "human nature" also refers to the kinds of beings we are. Materialism refers to the view that we are material beings who depend on a body in order to function. Dualism refers to the view that we are both mental things or souls and physical things, our bodies. Idealism says that we are spiritual beings. The creation story in Genesis 2 embraces materialism. We are physical things that God has made alive. Jesus and his followers clearly embraced the authority of the law and the prophets. They thus accepted the creation stories of Genesis 1 and 2.

In the Synoptic Gospels this materialistic bent is seen in their assumptions about the kingdom of God. The ideal kingdom was portrayed as a social world on earth, not an otherworldly heaven.

## ELEMENTS FOUR, FIVE, AND SIX

These elements refer to beliefs and assumption about rituals, authority, and the religious ultimate.

Judaism provided the context of the life of Jesus. He and all of his first followers were Jews. In Matthew and Luke his lineage is traced back to Abraham. His religious home and those of his first followers was the synagogue. As mentioned above, the authority of the Law and the Prophets was assumed. Moses, Isaiah, and Joel are quoted. Luke has Jesus saying, "Everything written about me in the law and the prophets and the psalms must be fulfilled" (Luke 24:44). Mathew has Jesus say, "Think not that I have come to abolish the law and the prophets; I have come not to abolish them but to fulfill them" (5:17).

Paul had a tricky dance to perform. He wanted Christians to reject the law, but accept the Scriptures where law was emphasized. He thus emphasized Abraham, but not Moses. He even said that law came to increase the trespass (Rom 5:20). The logic seems to be that grace is more appreciated and important when sin increases.

As the Christian movement grew, the Law and the Prophets were not always highly regarded. Marcion in the latter part of the second century rejected those Scripture and focused on the importance of Paul. Given Paul's negative view of law, it is understandable that someone could interpret him as rejecting the Law and the Prophets.

There were also Christian gnostics who were similar to Marcion. They regarded the God of Genesis 1 and 2 as an inferior being. They regarded salvation as liberating people from the materialistic world. Thus the acceptance and the authority of the Law and the Prophets were important. Their acceptance implied the acceptance and importance of the creation stories. The value claims of the two creation stories with respect to the material world were rejected by Marcion and the gnostics. The repeated claim of the first creation story, "It was good," became controversial and often rejected.

Note that the value orientation shaped the interpretation of element six. Element six is the "missing piece" whose shape is determined by the shape of the other pieces.

One of the watershed differences found in the Jewish Scriptures is the difference between a conservative view and the liberal view of the divine command theory. According to the liberal interpretation, one should do the will of God because God embodies the appropriate ideals of justice and righteousness. This was clearly emphasized in Amos and in many of the other prophets. The Yahwist, which has no laws, assumed a conservative view. God is seen to be free to command whatever he wishes and his commanding something makes it right. This is the tradition of Karl Barth. We also found it in Paul.

Is there anything in the Synoptics that sheds light on this issue? "The Sabbath was made for man, not man for the Sabbath." The liberal view that law is for the sake of human well-being is not consistent with the conservative view. If the point of the law is maximizing human well-being, then God is not free to command just anything.

What about Matthew's view that the person who tones down the least of these commandments will be least in the kingdom of heaven? It assumes that there is an authority that tells us what the commandments are. It also assumes that the person who rejects or tones down these commandments rejects this authority. The authority, of course, would be God. In Matthew we have Jesus on a mountain top replacing Moses. In the Torah, Moses represents the authority of God. In Matthew, Jesus represents the authority of God.

Let's remember Deuteronomy, however. According to Deuteronomy the law embodies wisdom, understanding, and righteousness (Deut 4:6–8). They are also the source of life and death, blessing, and curse (Deut 30:19). We cannot conclude, therefore, that just because Moses and Jesus represent the authority of God, the commandments have no logic or reason. They can still embody wisdom, righteousness and be a source of life and well-being.

What about rituals? In the Synoptics there are no other baptisms performed except those done by John the Baptist. John says that Jesus will baptize them by the Holy Spirit (Mark 1:8, Matt 1:11, Luke 3:16). Baptism is not discussed. However, at the very end of Matthew, the resurrected Jesus is portrayed as saying, "Go therefore and make disciples of all nations, baptizing them in the name of the Father and of the Son and the Holy Spirit" (28:19). An analogous passage in Luke says, "Repentance and forgiveness of sins should be preached in his name to all nations" (24:27). There is no mention of baptism here. This same author, however, has Peter preaching on the day of Pentecost, "Repent, and be baptized every one of you in the name of Jesus Christ for the forgiveness of sins" (Acts 2:38).

The last supper is found in Mark 14:22–25, Matthew 26:26–29, and Luke 22:17–19. None of these passages say that this is a practice that ought to be adopted as a ritual. It is not like the Matthew passage which says to go, make disciples, and baptize them. It is understandable, however, that the last supper was picked up as a ritual.

## SUMMARY

In chapter 8 we outlined the view of the gospel in Romans and examined Peter's views found in speeches early in Acts. In Peter's speeches repentance was emphasized and Jesus was referred to as a second Moses. Matthew's Sermon on the Mount fits the latter and all of the Synoptics emphasize law and repentance.

What is the heart of the differences between Paul and the Synoptic Gospels? For Paul law and human nature conflict with one another and the result is spiritual death. The answer to this problem is faith and living according to the Spirit. The Spirit brings life.

For the Synoptics law and human nature do not conflict. The law is a source of life. In Jesus God willed the good and the good is the source of life.

The message of the Synoptic Gospels is to repent, seek first the kingdom of God, and invest one's life as a disciple. At the heart of the kingdom lie the two greatest commandments and social justice.

Differences lie with respect to the understanding of law, the kingdom, and the nature of the ministry of Jesus. Mark has a more liberal perspective that becomes more conservative in the hands of Matthew.

# PART 3

Criticisms

# 10

# Christology

AN ANALYSIS OF THE nature of religious views of life was presented in chapter 3. Chapters 4 through 9 then applied that analysis to early Hinduism, Buddhism, biblical Judaism, and early Christianity. We saw how that analysis helped us understand these early religious traditions and the changes that took place in their development.

Two things are certain about what has been said so far. Some people will say that this analysis is not applicable to Zen Buddhism. Some will say that it is not applicable to Christianity. Zen, it will be said, has no doctrines, makes no truth claims; it makes no claims about what is right and wrong, good and bad. Christianity, some will say, has a view of Christ which is incompatible with the analysis of religion given here.

According to this book, a religious point of view ought to be judged in part by the values within it. For some Christians, however, the view is that Christ is the ultimate basis for judging our actions. It will be said that this theory has things upside down. Christ is the ultimate standard of what is right and wrong, good and bad. Normal moral reflection is irrelevant.

To say that Christ is the ultimate standard for determining what is right, wrong, good and bad is to begin with a principle of authority and make deductions from there. These Christologies can be called deductive. Accepting Christ becomes something like an axiom from which deductions are made. The alternatives are inductive. Here reasons and arguments play a role in accepting the figure of Jesus. Here use of the elements of religion is appropriate.

Part 3 — Criticisms

Besides the distinction between an inductive and deductive Christologies, there is a distinction between functional and an incarnational Christologies. First we will discuss functional Christologies and incarnational Christologies; we then will examine types of deductive Christologies. Finally, we will examine an inductive Christology.

The discussion of Zen will put off until the next chapter.

## FUNCTIONAL CHRISTOLOGIES

In the Old Testament God is portrayed as being analogous to a king. A king chooses, designates, elects, promises, anoints and adopts. One kind of Christology sees Jesus as the one who God chooses, designates, elects, promises, anoints or adopts in order to fulfill his purposes.

A function is a role Jesus is interpreted as playing in light of God's purposes. In the Synoptic Gospels the focus is on the kingdom of God. It is assumed that God's purpose is to bring creation to a fulfillment in an ideal kingdom—the kingdom of God. Functional Christologies see Jesus as playing a role with respect to this kingdom.

In the first speech attributed to Peter in Acts the resurrection is described as putting Jesus on a throne (Acts 2:30)—a form of anointing. In Luke's gospel Elizabeth has a vision in which she is told, "The Lord God will give to him [Jesus] the throne of his father David" (Luke 1:32).

What's going on here? In the Psalms and in the Prophets there is a vision of God eventually bringing about an ideal kingdom involving all nations and someone on David's throne (see 2 Sam 7:12–13; Ps 132:11–12; Dan 7:13–14). Talk of putting Jesus on David's throne is thus to link Jesus to the eventual establishment of God's ideal kingdom on earth—an emphasis found in all of the Synoptic Gospels. Since this kingdom embodies all of the values important to God, a functional Christology assumes the importance of this kingdom and the values embedded within it.

In Acts 13:33 the second psalm is quoted and applied to the resurrection. It says, "Thou art my Son, today I have begotten thee." Being adopted carries the implication of being chosen. This psalm then goes on to say, "Ask of me, and I will make the nations your heritage and the ends of the earth your possession." In other words, being an adopted son means that he could be the appointed ruler of a kingdom involving all nations. We have what Howard Clark Kee refers to as the imperial theology of the Roman Empire applied to the Christian faith.[1]

Functional Christologies assume the values embedded in the kingdom, but do not explicate them. They avoid the difficult metaphysical problems often tied to incarnational Christologies.

## INCARNATIONAL CHRISTOLOGIES

Incarnational Christologies take two different forms. Either God is pictured as being present in the figure of Jesus, or Jesus is portrayed as a preexisting being that became flesh. When Paul said, "God was in Christ reconciling the world unto himself" (2 Cor 5:19), he was saying that God was present and operative in this figure. This assumed the first type of incarnational Christology. This type of Christology sees God as revealing himself through Jesus.

In the Synoptic Gospels at his baptism when Jesus hears the voice say, "Thou art my Son," this is followed by the statement "with thee I am well pleased." In the last chapter it was pointed out that the verb used here is in the aorist tense. It thus refers to a happening or event in the past, an event which is for the good. "In thee I have willed the good" would be an appropriate translation. This would imply that the ministry of Jesus is to be understood as a product of the good that God has willed in him.

After his baptism Luke's gospel proceeds to have Jesus support this claim. It has Jesus at the beginning of his ministry stand up in a synagogue and read from the prophet Isaiah: "The Spirit of the Lord is upon me, because he has anointed me to preach good news to the poor" (Luke 4:18). In a sermon in Acts, Peter describes Jesus by saying, "How God anointed Jesus of Nazareth with the Holy Spirit and with power; how he went about doing good and healing all that were oppressed by the devil, for God was with him" (Acts 10:38). For the Spirit of the Lord or for the Holy Spirit to be upon a person is one way for God to be incarnate in a person.

Note that this kind of incarnation does not make God's presence in Jesus different significantly from what it can be in other individuals. God can be present and manifest himself in the life and actions of other individuals.

The other type of incarnational Christology is to regard Jesus as the manifestation of a preexisting being who became flesh. John's gospel begins, "In the beginning was the Word, and the Word was with God, and

---

1. Kee, *Jesus in History*, 115.

the Word was God . . . And the Word became flesh and dwelt among us" (John 1:1, 14). There has been much discussion about the word "God" in the phrase "the Word was God." The question is whether the word "divine" should be used here. If not, the question is whether the sentence makes any sense. In the background of this discussion stands the Nicene Creed which favors the use of the word "God" here.

This type of Christology is also in Philippians 2:5–11 and in Colossians 1:15–19. It should be noted that in both of these letters the phrase "Jesus Christ" functions as a name. This differs from the Synoptic Gospels where "Christ" functions as a title. In Mark's gospel, in the eighth chapter, Peter came to recognized Jesus as the Christ—as the promised Messiah.

In this type of incarnational Christology two questions are relevant. What relationship does the preexisting being have to God, and to what extent does this being become a man?

Colossians 1:15–19 says of Jesus Christ, "He is the image of the invisible God, the first-born of all creation; for in him all things were created . . . For in him all the fullness of God was pleased to dwell." Note that it says that this being was created. This differs from the Logos in John's gospel which says that in the beginning the Logos was with God.

Later Paul refers to this being as having a body of flesh and as dying (Col 1:22). If Jesus Christ is the first to be created, it makes sense to say that he could die.

What about the question as to whether he was a real human being. Having flesh would not require that he be a human being. Dying may be regarded as indicating that he is human, but it can also be explained by the fact that he was created. What Paul says in Colossians is consistent with what he says in Philippians, where he says that this being was born "in the likeness of men" (Phil 2:7).

In Paul's Letter to the Philippians, he says,

> Have this mind among yourselves, which you have in Christ Jesus, who, though he was in the form of God, did not count equality with God a thing to be grasped, but emptied himself, taking the form of a servant, being born in the likeness of men. And being found in the human form he humbled himself and became obedient unto death, even death on a cross. (Phil 2:5–8)

This kind of Christology is referred to as a kenotic Christology. It is based on the Greek word for emptying—*ikinosin*.

Here we have a preexisting figure that is in the form of God but does not grasp after equality with God. Presumably a contrast is being drawn between this figure and an analogous figure who grasped after equality with God. The devil might be that individual. Since he is portrayed as not choosing to grasp after equality with God, the assumption is that he is not equal to God. Nevertheless, he embodies the ideal that God purportedly would have humans embrace—the ideal of being servants of one another. We thus have incarnation in the first sense, because God's will is being portrayed, and also incarnation in the second sense.

Paul does not say that this person was a human being but had the likeness of one and the form of one.

If Jesus were merely a preexisting being who took on a human form, this would not be enough to make him religiously significant for Christians. The world of the first two centuries was populated with many beings of this type. There had to be something unique about him. This was either serving in a special function, or manifesting God's will, or doing something for us on the cross.

A Christology which claims that the will of God may be known through Jesus can be defended by defending the values that were present in his ministry. This is the first kind of incarnational Christology. It can take the form of an inductive Christology.

A person who sees the elements of religion as incompatible with a proper Christology will assume a deductive Christology. There have been at least three versions: the Christology found in John's gospel, the Christology embedded in the creeds of Nicaea and Chalcedon, and the Christology in Barth's theology.

## CHRISTOLOGY IN JOHN'S GOSPEL

In the Gospel of John we find a strong emphasis on authority. Jesus is portrayed as representing the authority of God the Father. John 12:49–50 says, "For I have not spoken on my own authority; the Father who sent me has himself given me commandment what to say and what to speak. And I know that his commandment is eternal life. What I say, therefore, I say as the Father has bidden me."

In this gospel Jesus is presented as asserting the following:

1. He has come from the Father who is in heaven (5:23, 36; 6:38; 8:29, 42; 10:36; 12:49; 16:28).
2. His coming was not his idea (7:28; 8:42).
3. He can do nothing on his own authority (5:30; 8:28).
4. He is doing and saying what his Father told him to do and say (4:34; 5:36; 6:38; 7:16; 8:28; 12:50).
5. He who does not honor the Son does not honor the Father who sent him (5:23).
6. And, because of the above, people should accept him and obey him.

The conclusion reached here is underlined when Jesus says of himself, "No one comes to the Father, but by me" (14:6).

This is radically different from what we find in Mark's gospel, the earliest gospel. There Jesus doesn't even make a public proclamation that he is the Christ. He tells his disciples not to say anything about this (Mark 8:30).

How come this emphasis on authority? Two things should be noted. First, representing Jesus as having that authority is one way of granting the church power and authority. The church is understood to be the representative of Christ on earth. In John 20:23, Jesus is described as saying to his followers, "If you forgive the sins of any, they are forgiven; if you retain the sins of any, they are retained." Such a statement assumes that Jesus represents the authority of God; it also gives to the church the authority to forgive sins.

Second, authority is likely to be asserted when the character of faith is called into question. For a while after the death of Jesus all of the followers of Jesus were Jews who met in synagogues. The Jesus followers were like a sect within Judaism which Paul expanded. This gospel differs from Mark and Matthew because it makes constant reference to "the Jews." A divorce is sought or has taken place. The Jews who identify with Jesus no longer consider themselves Jews. The Jewish faith gave birth to a bunch of Jesus followers. These children have started to grow up. They are like rebellious teenagers. In fact, at one point in John, Jesus refers to Jews as children of the devil (8:44).

In John 16:2–3, Jesus is described as saying to his disciples: "They will put you out of the synagogues; indeed, the hour is coming when whoever kills you will think he is offering service to God. And they will do this because they have not known the Father, nor me." A similar reference is also found in John 9:22. Religious fights tend to be hot. These references are unique to John's gospel. They suggest that this was written at a time later than the other gospels, when this was happening. This would suggest that the divorce was in the process of taking place.

Traditionally John has been dated later than the other gospels because of use of the phrase "the Jews" and the attitude it takes toward Jews. Marcus Borg has pointed out, however, that Acts also has many references to "the Jews"—13:50; 14:1–6, 19; 17:1–5; 18:12; 20:3; 21:27–36; 22:22; 23:12–14; 24:5–9; and 25:7. Whereas Luke-Acts is often dated in the 80s, he dates it in the second century.

## CHRISTOLOGY OF CHALCEDON

The Gospel of John has Jesus say that he is saying what his Father wanted him to say. What if the Son did not properly understand what the Father told him or forgot much of it? Here we can understand some of the logic behind the creeds of Nicaea and Chalcedon. If Jesus were fully God, then there could be no communication problem. Both would be omniscient. People often want their faith based on a foundation that is absolutely certain.

Of these two creeds Chalcedon is the most important because it endorses Nicaea and builds upon it. It says,

> Therefore, following the holy fathers, we all with one accord teach men to acknowledge one and the same Son, our Lord Jesus Christ, at once complete in Godhead and complete in manhood, truly God and truly man, consisting also of a reasonable soul and body; of one substance with the Father as regards his Godhead, and at the same time of one substance with us as regards his manhood; like us in all respects, apart from sin; as regards his Godhead, begotten of the Father before the ages, but yet as regards his manhood begotten, for us men and for our salvation, of Mary the Virgin, the God-bearer; one and the same Christ, Son, Lord, Only-begotten, recognized in two natures, without confusion, without change, without division, without separation; the distinction of natures being in no way annulled by the union, but rather the characteristics of each nature being preserved and coming together to form one person and subsistence, not as parted or separated into two persons, but one and the same Son and Only-begotten God the Word, Lord Jesus Christ; even as the prophets from earliest times

spoke of him, and our Lord Jesus Christ himself taught us, and the creed of the fathers has handed down to us.[2]

To understand this creed one must put it in its context. Christian theology had come upon the scene. One of the most influential ones was Origen of Alexandria (185–254 CE) who reworked Neo-Platonism. He perceived Christ as an emanation from the ultimate, the Father, and the Holy Spirit as a second emanation.

Constantine, the Roman emperor from 306–337, became a Christian, and a marriage resulted between the Roman Empire and the church. At that time there were fights in the Empire over the issue of Christology which he wanted to end. The emperor thus calls the bishops to solve the problem—assuming that they had the power and authority to make peace. They had power, but they didn't resolve the controversy.

In the fights over Christology, each school of thought could justify itself by appealing to something in the New Testament. The only backing the bishops had was an appeal to the New Testament. Religious traditions don't like to reject popular views. Put in their context Mark's gospel is radically different from John's gospel. But the creeds sought to combine the manhood of Jesus in Mark's gospel, the birth stories in Matthew and Luke, and the incarnation story of John's gospel. The latter we have seen identified Christ with the divine Logos that was in the beginning with God.

How the Chalcedon Creed is weighed depends in part upon how much authority a person gives to the New Testament and how much authority is granted to the bishops. Denial of this creed is sometimes grounds for being excommunicated from a church.

On the contemporary scene the prime issue seems to be whether the putting together of the various parts of the New Testament into a creed resulted in something logically consistent. Is Jesus to be understood as both omniscient and very limited in knowledge; as omnipotent and very limited in power? Is this logically consistent?

The importance of the problem accelerated with the publication in 1977 of the book *The Myth of God Incarnate*, edited by John Hick. That book generated a significant amount of heated discussion. It is beyond the scope of this chapter to summarize that material and assess it. Hick has done a good job of covering that material in his book *The Metaphor of God Incarnate*. A person may not agree with his conclusions but nevertheless he does a good job of covering the waterfront.

2. CRTA, "Definition of the Council of Chalcedon."

It is important to understand that the title, *The Myth of God Incarnate*, was intended as double entendre. For David Straus (1807–1874) myths are stories about the past which aim to convey truths, but not literal truths about what happened. From this perspective, the myth of the incarnation may convey truth but not a literal truth. Hick's book *The Metaphor of God Incarnate* is in that tradition. Myth, of course, can also refer to falsehood. Many who read the book understood it that way. Michael Green's book *The Truth of God Incarnate* (1977) was a quick response to Hick's book to defend a literal interpretation of the incarnation. He regarded it as an attack on fundamental Christian faith.

The most popular defense of a literal interpretation is to use a kenotic Christology. According to these theories God the Son, the second person of the Trinity who is omniscient and omnipotent, empties himself, as in Philippians 2:5–8. He becomes a true human being. He empties himself of omniscience and omnipotence. Does this make sense? Could Jesus still serve the role of revealing God and giving us guidance as to what God would have us do?

Ronald Feenstra's paper "Reconsidering Kenotic Christology" is a sophisticated interpretation of this theory. He points out that the critics of the kenotic theory say that when the Son becomes a human being he would have to give up his essential divine attributes. He thus would not be God in the flesh. He would have been God in the past and omniscient in the past, but not during his lifetime. Jesus would thus not be God in the flesh.

Does it make sense, however, to say that God could cease to be God? The question is about what is required to be God; about what is essential to be God.

Feenstra suggests an answer to that question with respect to omniscience. He suggests a way that Jesus could be truly a human being and also at the same time divine and omniscient. He suggests that God could have the essential divine property of omniscience-unless-kenotically-incarnate. With that as an essential property, he says that Jesus could be a true human being and at the same time omniscient in this sense.

A problem here is that "kenotically-incarnate" is a technical piece of jargon that needs to be unpacked. Clearly whatever is kenotically incarnate is not omniscient. Could we say that it is a divine property of God to be omniscient unless not omniscient? The problem is that all of us are omniscient unless not omniscient. For the concept of being kenotically incarnate to be a useful concept, it has to refer to something other than just not being omniscient.

There is another problem here. To be a human being is to have human freedom and to be really capable of sinning. If Jesus is complete in Godhood and complete in manhood, then God would have to be really capable of sinning. Should a Christian say that God is really capable of sinning?

There is a long tradition going back to the prophets such as Amos, Isaiah, and Jeremiah which emphasized that God is essentially good. We have seen that this is assumed in the Synoptic Gospels. On the other hand, where a conservative view of the divine command theory is assumed, God is then free to command whatever he wishes and no necessity is tied to what is good or right. We found this in the Yahwist and in Paul's view of election in the ninth chapter of Romans. I suggest that it is foolish to deny that God is necessarily good. One denies the best in the Hebrew and early Christian traditions.

## KARL BARTH'S CHRISTOLOGY

Karl Barth has a different kind of deductive Christology. He says that Jesus Christ is to be understood as revelation. He uses the phrase "self-revelation" and refers to this as "the basic text" that the apostles read and expanded upon.[3] It is, he says, the work of Christian theology to continually expand on this text.

Since he does not practice biblical criticism nor refer to those who do, the question arises as to whether "Jesus Christ" functions for him as symbol as it does for Tillich. He says, however, this: "If it [Jesus Christ] were a principle and not a name indicating a person, we should describe it as the epistemological principle of the message."[4] "Jesus Christ" thus refers to a person. Epistemology is the study of how to find knowledge. He thus wants to say that knowledge in Christian theology is to be understood in terms of revelation and Jesus Christ is that revelation.

Two questions now arise: What does Barth mean by revelation and how is it related to the historical Jesus?

---

3. Barth, *Dogmatics*, IV/2, 122.
4. Ibid., IV/1, 17.

"Revelation," Barth says, "is the truth besides which there is no other truth, over against which there is only lying and wrong."[5] He also says that it is the act of a free and sovereign God. The traditional view is that revelation is an act of God making known propositional truths. That clearly does not apply here. That leaves open the question of what it is.

Since our knowledge of Jesus comes through the gospels and they present different views of Jesus, the question arises as to whether it is Matthew's Jesus or Mark's Jesus. We saw that they differ with respect to their understanding of law and their view of the mission of Jesus. One had a strict view of law and the other a liberal. One had a limited view of Jesus' mission and the other didn't.

Linked to revelation, he says, is faith. "The activity which corresponds to revelation would have to be faith: the recognition of the self-offering and self-manifestation of God."[6] As odd as it may seem, Barth draws a contrast between faith and religion. He says,

> Because it is grasping, religion is the contradiction of revelation, the concentrated expression of human unbelief, i.e., an attitude and activity which is directly opposed to faith. It is a feeble but defiant, an arrogant but hopeless, attempt to create something which man could do, but now cannot do, or can do only because and if God himself creates it for him: the knowledge of the truth, the knowledge of God.[7]

Note that Barth says here that God creates for the individual knowledge of the truth and knowledge of God. He also says that knowledge in Christian theology is to be understood in terms of revelation and Jesus Christ is that revelation. If God creates the knowledge of God, then one wonders whether a Jew by the name of Jesus could be that revelation. "Jesus" refers to a particular with a set of qualities.

Why should we consider Jesus as the definitive revelation of God? For Barth to pose this question is to misunderstand the nature of revelation. Revelation, he wishes to say, is the act of a free and sovereign God. To use standards to determine what is revelatory is to base faith on human reason, which is self-exultation. It is to define God in terms of human beings, instead of defining human beings in terms of God.

---

5. 52 Ibid., I/2, 325.
6. Ibid., 301.
7. Ibid., 302–3.

What we have here is a conservative view of the divine command theory. We found this view in our analysis of the early biblical tradition in the early Yahwist source. We also found it in Paul's Letter to the Romans, chapter 9:14–18. According to this view God is free to command anything and his commanding something makes it right. For Barth, Christ represents an action, a revelation of a free and sovereign being. His choosing to reveal himself is what makes it to be right. There is no knowledge of God apart from God's revelation of it, and people are basically ignorant of God except when they respond in faith and accept revelation as he understands it.

What gets lost here is the Jewish fella named "Jesus." What we have instead is a free and sovereign God who is free to make commands and reveal himself and makes himself known as he sees fit.

One problem here is that there is no reason for thinking that Barth's view is true. Another problem is that the approach used here opens the door to all kinds of religious garbage, moral atrocities, and religious fanaticism. Reason has no role to get rid of the garbage. Appealing to God's commands has been used to justify the killing of men, women and children in city after city. At the same time it is used to justify keeping cattle for booty (Josh 6:21; 8:1–2).

A third problem lies in the fact that our knowledge of Jesus is dependent upon the New Testament. We have four gospels with different views of Jesus, his teachings, and his ministry. If we are talking about the historical Jesus then we have to take seriously the only sources we have. We have to take historical criticism seriously—the work of scholars such as Albert Schweitzer and Bart Ehrman.

Since our knowledge of Jesus is dependent on the four gospels the question arises as to whether those gospels rely upon authority, as Barth would have us do, or whether they emphasize reasons and arguments? If some of the gospels emphasize reason and arguments, it would be odd to focus exclusively on authority.

## AN INDUCTIVE CHRISTOLOGY

An inductive Christology begins by assuming a liberal version of the divine command theory. This is to say that a person ought to do the will of God because God embodies the most important moral principles such as goodness, righteousness, and justice. These three were emphasized by Amos.

Such a theory then looks at the Synoptic Gospels and finds in the ministry of Jesus, in the things he said and did, principles in this tradition that deserve to be defended.

In the second chapter of Mark Jesus is portrayed as eating with the social and religious outcastes—tax collectors and sinners—for which he is criticized. The response of Jesus is to recognize the ideal of the physician who is committed to healing those who have needs. "Those who are well have no need of a physician," he says, "but those who are sick" (Mark 2:17). Note we have a subtle argument, a reason. Later his disciples are criticized for not keeping the Sabbath when plucking grain while walking through grain fields. His response is, "The Sabbath was made for man, not man for the Sabbath" (Mark 2:27). A view of the law is implied here which gives primacy to human beings and their needs. This would seem to follow from the love commandment being the most important one. In the next chapter, Jesus is portrayed as entering a synagogue on the Sabbath where there is a man with a withered hand. When he is about to be criticized for healing on the Sabbath, a form of work, he responds with an argument: "Is it lawful on the Sabbath to do good or to do harm, to save life or to kill?" (Mark 3:4).

In other words, arguments are used here to defend a view of the law which emphasizes the primacy of human beings and their needs. In other words, Mark's gospel seeks to justify and convince us of the importance of what Jesus said and did. This is an inductive Christology.

If God embodies the most important moral principles and if those principles are found in the ministry of Jesus and in the things he said and did, then God was present in that ministry and in some of the things he said and did. This involves the first type of incarnational Christology.

## SUMMARY

At the beginning of this chapter it was said that some Christians would reject the analysis of religion presented in chapter 3 because this analysis says that a religious understanding of life ought to be judged in part by the values embedded in it. Some critics will say that theory has things turned upside down. What is right and wrong, good and bad ought to be determined by reference to Christ.

We have seen that Christologies fall into four categories: functional, incarnational, inductive, and deductive. These categories are not exclusive of one another. John's gospel has both an incarnational Christology and a deductive Christology. The Synoptic Gospels emphasize a functional Christology where reasons and arguments are sometimes found; that is, they take an inductive form. The Synoptic Gospels sometimes also have the first type of incarnational Christology. This is one where God is portrayed as present and operative in the figure of Jesus. For example, where Jesus is described as saying, "The Spirit of the Lord is upon me" (Luke 4:18).

Those who reject the view of religion found in this book because of Christology will have a deductive Christology. Deductive Christologies appeal to some form of authority and then make deductions from there. The first form of this is found in John's gospel—the last of the gospels to be written. It takes place in the context of a heated divorce taking place between Jews and Christians. One spouse was attacking the other spouse.

Later a group of bishops, who identified with this gospel, chose to bond with the Roman Empire. Instead of a divorce, there was here a kind of marriage. This marriage gave birth to the Chalcedon Creed. To understand John's gospel and the Chalcedon Creed requires understanding the social and political forces behind them. There would be no Gospel of John without a conflict between Jews and Christians. There would have been no Chalcedon Creed without an emperor adopting the Christian faith; and then calling together a group of bishops to resolve the fights over Christology that permeated much of the Roman Empire. This is not to make a theological assessment of the gospel or of Chalcedon, but to describe reality.

The world of the fourth century, where we find Chalcedon and Nicaea, is radically different from the world of the first-century Christians. The interest was not in Jesus the Jew. The interest was in reworking John's gospel. It is the nature of religious traditions not to reject popular traditions belonging to the past, but to add on to them and seek to combine them in one way or another. Put in their context Mark's gospel is radically different from John's gospel. But the creeds sought to combine the manhood of Jesus in Mark's gospel, the birth stories in Matthew and Luke, and the incarnation story of John's gospel.

An important question for those who identify with Chalcedon is the question of whether Chalcedon was logically consistent in its search to put together these various traditions. The most popular way of defending Chalcedon is to embrace a kenotic Christology. This is based on Philippians which says that Christ Jesus had the form of God and then emptied himself and took upon a human form (Phil 2:5–8).

## CHRISTOLOGY

Ronald Feenstra gives a sophisticated interpretation of this kind of Christology. The problem is that if Jesus is fully human, then he is not omniscient. If he is fully God, then he is omniscient. Feenstra suggests that God could have the essential quality of being omniscient-unless-kenotically-incarnate. "Kenotically-incarnate" is a technical notion which implies a lack of omniscience. The problem is to explicate this notion without reducing it to a trivial notion of being non-omniscient. We are all omniscient unless non-omniscient.

Another problem: If Jesus was fully human then there was a real possibility of sinning. If he were also fully God, then God has the real possibility of sinning. The argument here is that this gives up too much that is important to the Jewish and early Christian tradition. In the prophets God is perceived as essentially good and thus they rejected many of the norms found in the Yahwist. This was also assumed in the Synoptic Gospels. Unfortunately it is rejected by Paul in the ninth chapter of Romans. In both the Yahwist and in Paul God is free to command anything. God is not necessarily good but whatever he happens to choose is good. The suggestion here is that one ought not to give up the notion that God is essentially good in order to preserve Chalcedon.

Rather than discuss the problem of two natures, Barth just regards Jesus Christ as the definitive revelation of God. The proper response to this revelation, he says, is faith.

We have seen that there are three problems here. First, why should anyone regard Jesus this way? Barth has no answer to this.

Second, this opens the door to all kinds of moral garbage as we find in the sixth and eighth chapters of Joshua. The Israelites are described as killing all men, women, children, and cattle in city after city in response to God's command.

The third problem is based on the fact that our knowledge of Jesus is dependent on the four gospels which have different views of Jesus. An inductive Christology can recognize multiplicity and opt for those principles and teachings that are the most reasonable.

# 11

# Zen Buddhism

IN CHAPTER 4 IT was suggested that religious views of life involve beliefs and assumptions that fall into six categories. They include beliefs and assumptions about values, happiness, human nature, rituals, authority, and a sixth category which includes beliefs about God, the gods, Nirvana, and the Buddha-Body. Priority is to be given to beliefs about values and what is called spiritual hypotheticals. The latter refer to views about wherein lie the happiness and well-being of individuals and the society, as well as their deterioration. Views of human fulfillment make assumptions about human nature, which is the third category. Beliefs and assumptions about values, spiritual hypotheticals and human nature are beliefs and assumptions that everyone has. They are thus referred to as the elements of life. Priority is given to them, even though sometimes beliefs about priests (element four) and authority (element five) can play an important role.

The implication here is that religion is about concerns that everyone has. We are all concerned about the things that are important. We are all concerned about happiness and well-being. Religious views of life are just more expansive in that they include something that falls into the sixth category. Interpretations of elements four and five are sometimes present, but are not necessary. When present, they may not affect interpretations of elements one, two and three. Priests and rituals may just be pragmatic and useful. Authority may be accepted because of the truth embedded in interpretation of the other elements.

## ZEN BUDDHISM

A religious view of life is like a puzzle made of six pieces. Through experience and reflections upon experience we learn about values, spiritual hypotheticals, views of human nature. We can appeal to experience and reflections upon experience to critique views of authority and rituals. The question then arises as to how beliefs and assumptions about God, the gods, and Nirvana fit into this puzzle. The size and shape of this piece is determined by the size and shape of other pieces. We saw, for example, how a shift in values and spiritual hypotheticals resulted in a shift from the gods of the early Rig Veda to the recognition of Brahman in the Upanishads. A shift in values also took place in Buddhism when the *Prajna-paramita sutrass* started to come upon the scene. Those Sutras affected Buddhism as it developed in China, which included the development of Zen Buddhism.

What follows from this view of religion is a view about the role and function of theology. Its role is to present, defend and criticize interpretations of the six elements of religion.

We are first going to examine objections to this view of religion from a Zen Buddhist perspective. This will be followed by an outsider's view of the nature Rinzai Zen. It is always appropriate to stand outside of a religious tradition to seek to understand it. This outsider's view will make use of interpretations of the elements of religion. Finally, a reply will be given to those who say that the elements of religion do not apply to Zen.

## OBJECTIONS TO THE ELEMENTS OF RELIGION

A person in the tradition of Zen is going to object by saying that Zen does not have a theology and does not believe it ought to have a theology. Theology, it will be said, involves theory. Attachment to theory in the context of religion is a basic human problem—a problem from which we need to be liberated. A famous statement of the faith of Zen says, "A special transmission outside the Scriptures; No dependence upon words and letters." Any attempt to capture the truth of Zen by means of a set of statements, it will be said, would tie the truth of Zen to a set of words and letters. It would thus embody a misunderstanding of what Zen is.

What follows is the necessity of a Zen master to convey an understanding of Zen by direct transmission. What is conveyed cannot be captured by a set of statements.

A second objection relates to the importance this view of religion gives to values. Values involve notions about the things that are good and bad, right and wrong. An early Zen poem tells us, "Be not concerned with right and wrong. The conflict between right and wrong is the sickness of the mind."[1] It is not just the conflict between moral values that is looked down upon. Alan Watts puts the point this way:

> To see . . . good without evil is like up without down, and that to make an ideal of pursuing the good is like trying to get rid of the left by turning constantly to the right. One is therefore compelled to go around in circles . . . how hard it is to think in any other terms than good or bad, or a muddy mixture of the two. Yet Zen is a liberation from this pattern, and its apparently dismal starting point is to understand the absurdity of choosing, of the whole feeling that life may be significantly improved by a constant selection of the good.[2]

Besides this, note should be taken that resentment exists among Zen Buddhists of being told by outsiders what the meaning of Zen is. A director of a Zen institute in Japan—who has been a Zen Buddhist for twenty-five years—reflects this attitude when she says, "How many hours have I not spend in my Kyoto temple listening to people, usually Americans recently come to Japan, tell me just what Zen is. To such visitors I have nothing to say."[3]

## THE ORIGINS OF ZEN

To understand Zen it will help to look at its own story of its origins. Zen tradition traces its roots to a sermon presented by Sakyamuni (Gautama) at the Mount of the Holy Vulture. On that occasion, without saying anything, he merely held up a bouquet of flowers given to him by a lay disciple. End of sermon. Only one disciple, Mahakasyapa, is said to have understood this. He showed this by quietly smiling at the Master. Sakyamuni replied, "I have the most precious treasure, spiritual and transcendental, which this moment I hand over to you, O venerable Mahakasyapa!"[4]

Zen Buddhism recognizes in each generation the presence of a master or patriarch who embodies the authority of the religious tradition. It is this authority that was being handed over to Mahakasyapa on this special

---

1. Watts, *Way of Zen*, 116.
2. Ibid., 116–17.
3. Sasaki, "Zen," 17.
4. Suzuki, *Zen Buddhism*, 59.

occasion. A master certifies the authenticity of particular realizations of enlightenment and determines who will be his successor. Beginning with Sakyamuni and the Mahakasyapa, Zen tradition recognizes twenty-eight patriarchs in India. The twenty-eighth one, Bodhidharma, is given credit for bringing the tradition to China in 520 CE. Tradition sums up his teaching in the following verse: "A special transmission outside the scriptures; No dependence upon words and letters; Direct pointing at the soul of man; Seeing into one's nature and the attainment of Buddhahood."[5]

Besides this verse, Bodhidharma is also known for another expression of faith. On one occasion Emperor Wu is said to have asked him, "What is the first principle of the holy doctrine?" Bodhidharma replied, "Vast emptiness, and there is nothing in it to be called holy."[6]

## PRAJNA-PARAMITA SUTRAS

The notion of a transmission outside of scripture and this emphasis on emptiness reflect the influence of the *Prajna-paramita sutras*. The philosophy found there is referred to as Madhyamika. These scriptures are the major identifying mark of the Mahayana tradition to which Zen belongs. They came upon the scene between about 100 BCE and 400 CE.

These sutras (discourses) portray dialogues with the Sakyamuni. They present a set of ideals to which a bodhisattva is committed—a course of life open to all and to which all should aspire. One of them tells us, "A Bodhisattva should become one whose thought is directed toward the benefit and ease of all beings."[7] He should say to himself,

> For the sake of each single being I will experience four hundreds of thousands of niyutas of kotis of aeons the pains of the hells, of the animal world, of the world of Yama, until those beings have won Nirvana in the realm of Nirvana which leaves nothing behind.[8]

According to these sutras, wisdom leads not only to acts that benefit all beings, but also to the recognition of the emptiness of what are referred to as "dharmas." According to early Buddhism, dharmas are phenomenal realities directly present in experience. They are considered to be the basic

---

5. Ibid., 61.
6. Ibid., 64.
7. *Large Sutra*, 125.
8. Ibid., 124.

elements of which this world is composed. This world was permeated with sorrow and suffering. Attachment to these dharmas was the source of sorrow and suffering.

Eighty-three types of dharmas were recognized. Calling them empty functioned to call into question the assumption that dharma-language can capture the nature and character of reality. It also functioned to alter people's attitudes toward nature and the social and political world in which they live. It is important to understand both of these functions.

To call these dharmas empty was to consider them to be "adventitious designations," a phrase used in these sutras. To call them adventitious designations meant that they were merely a product of human invention. The view is that the language, the dharma language used to classify and capture the nature of the reality, has no justification. It is not grounded in the nature of reality. That language is mere language and nothing exists to justify it.

Added to this, however, was the claim that language can have a legitimate practical function. Language can be used as a skillful means of helping us through life. It just cannot tell us what life is about; cannot tell us about the nature of reality. A Bodhisattva is thus portrayed as one who is skilled in means.

The Buddha is portrayed as diagnosing the problem when he says, "Names and signs are sources of attachment."[9] We get attached to names and signs and think that because we have them we have Truth and Reality. This is an illusion. The person who sets out for enlightenment and attends to signs will become attached. With attachment comes no enlightenment.

The assumption that language cannot capture the nature of reality leads naturally to the belief that the content of religion must be conveyed by a special transmission outside of the scriptures. There is to be no dependence upon words and letters. These are claims that tradition attributes to Bodhidharma when he brought Zen to China.

If language cannot capture the nature of reality, what then about the distinction between Samsara and Nirvana? Theravada Buddhism sees ultimate liberation as escape from Samsara and entrance into Nirvana. The *Prajna-paramita sutras* at this point take what will seem to be a rather shocking move. They consider this distinction to be empty. The distinction can have practical usefulness, used skillfully, but the distinction does not tell us anything about reality.

9. Ibid., 298.

## Zen Buddhism

The traditional metaphor used to portray Samsara and Nirvana is that there are two shores—the close shore being Samsara and the further shore being Nirvana. The passage from one shore to the other is said to be by a ferry boat. The boat itself involves the teachings of Siddhartha and the community of the monks, the sangha.

A Prajna-paramita sutras tells us that perfection of wisdom "is not on the shore this side, or on the shore beyond, or in between the two."[10] Why? The answer: "Because of its absolute purity." The flip side of the fact that our ordinary distinctions are empty is the fact that the perfection of wisdom is absolutely pure. This means that unlike the dharmas it involves no distinctions and dichotomies.

The notion of emptiness also serves a second function—the function of changing people's attitudes toward the things of this world. In early Buddhism dharmas were the phenomenal constituents of this world. They were also understood as infected by sorrow, suffering and transitoriness. Among them were the transitory constituents of human existence, the five skandhas—body, feeling, conception, dispositions, and consciousness. All of these dharmas were valued negatively. The only hope was to escape from this realm of Samsara and enter Final Nirvana. To claim that these dharmas are empty is to claim that they lacked their own being, to claim that they were false reifications. They were not something to be shunned or feared. Since the distinction between Samsara and Nirvana is empty there is no need to escape from Samsara. Robinson and Johnson express it this way:

> The bodhisattva can work and play in the secular world without fear of contamination from sense objects, because he knows that intrinsically they are neither pure nor impure. He associates with merchants, kings, harlots, and drunkards without falling into avarice, arrogance, lust, or dissipation. He accepts and excels in the arts and sciences, welcoming them as good means to benefit and edify living beings. He recognizes the religious capacities of women, listening respectfully when they preach the Dharma, because he knows that maleness and femaleness are both empty.[11]

When people take a very positive attitude toward the things of this world and have dispositions to support this attitude, they are valuing the things of this world. They are regarding them as being good. We do not want to say that Zen Buddhists refer to the things around us as having positive

---

10. Ibid.
11. Robinson and Johnson, *Buddhist Religion*, 70.

value. As outsiders, however, we are forced to say that they value positively the things of this world and life within society. Rejecting the language of valuing is not to reject the activity of valuing.

## RINZAI ZEN

This doctrine of emptiness and the value shift that went with it helped prepare the way for an emphasis in Zen that is not found in the *Prajnaparamita sutras*. The last two lines of the verse attributed to Bodhidharma say, "Direct pointing at the soul of man, seeing into one's nature and the attainment of Buddhahood." The implication here is that enlightenment is a matter of seeing into one's own nature—a nature referred to as a Buddha-nature. "Seeing into one's own nature"—D.T. Suzuki says of this phrase that it is the most significant one ever coined in the development of Zen Buddhism.[12]

It should be noted that there are a number of schools of Zen Buddhism. Hsu Yun is credited with reviving Zen in China, but most forms of Buddhism are linked to Japan where there are three schools or what might be called sects: Rinzai, Soto and Obaku. Obaku is by far the smallest. We are going to focus on the Rinzai School and rely primarily on Suzuki's exposition of it. Alan Watts, who has written much about Zen, has been influenced by Suzuki. In his book *Does It Matter* he dedicates a chapter to him. A major difference between the Rinzai School and the Soto School is the latter emphasizes meditation. Rinzai rejects meditation.

What does "seeing into one's nature" mean? Even though tradition ascribes this phrase to Bodhidharma, Suzuki doubts the historical accuracy of this. He thinks that if the phrase was used by him at all, he would not have understood it as it was understood in later Zen. Suzuki considers Hui-neng, the sixth patriarch in China, to be the real founder of Zen.

He based this on three principle ideas important to Rinzai. Hui-neng drew a contrast between seeing into one's nature and the practice of these trances. Bodhidharma emphasized these trances. He reflects the tradition of Theravada Buddhism and also the tradition of Soto Zen. Hui-neng considered the practice of meditative trances to be a mere matter of mental tranquilization.

Here we have a dispute over the appropriate type of spiritual hypothetical.

12. Suzuki, *Zen*, 74.

A second idea important to Hui-neng was that this seeing into one's own nature is an abrupt experience. Suzuki describes it this way: "An instant act in as far as the mental eye takes in the whole truth at one glance—the truth which transcends dualism in all form; it is abrupt as far as it knows no gradations, no continuous unfolding."[13] There are levels of trance and higher levels are achieved as one practices meditation. A person, however, either has seen into one's own nature or hasn't. Seeing into it is an event that happens all at once.

Hui-neng's third important idea is that the abrupt seeing into one's self-nature is a seeing of Self-Nature in the midst of its working and functioning. In other words, Self-Nature is something dynamic and seeing into it is not analogous to a meditative trance which is characterized by tranquility. This Self-Nature is referred to as the Buddha-Nature.

What is this Self-Nature, this Buddha-Nature?

## A MODEL OF RINZAI ZEN

To understand this Self-Nature, this Buddha-Nature, a model is appropriate. A model is a picture or representation of something that directs our way of perceiving that thing. If Y is a model to help us understand X, then a significant analogy should exist between Y and X. Looking at X as Y should then shed light upon X. H2-O is water, but a model for water would not be water but help us to understand it. A good model will shed light that helps us to properly perceive something.

According to our model of Rinzai Zen it should be perceived as a form of naturalism that embraces the following tenets:

1. All of reality is an interrelated unified system involving ourselves and everything that we observe around us.

2. That reality is something to be enjoyed and to be attuned to.

3. If one becomes responsive to one's inner nature, one becomes attuned to reality as a whole. Life will then become alive, spontaneous, free, and in harmony with the whole.

4. In the context of religion, to pursue goals or to commit oneself to a life of the mind and to thoughtful problem solving leads to spiritual death. It leads to self-destruction and to disharmony with the whole.

13. Ibid., 75.

5. One can become attuned to oneself and Nature by means of an abrupt experience referred to as satori.

The first statement is a metaphysical statement that expresses a view of what naturalism is. Nothing in our analysis of religion rules out the possibility of Nature functioning as a religious ultimate.

The second statement is a value judgment. It does not say that nature is called good but a positive attitude is taken toward it. The third and fourth statements are both spiritual hypotheticals. One is a view of wherein lies the source of life and well-being. The other is a view of wherein lies the source of spiritual death. The fifth statement characterizes the nature of the experience that leads a person to be responsive to one's inner nature and to be attuned to Nature.

Let us consider each of these statements one at a time. For our interpretation of Zen we will rely heavily on the work of D. T. Suzuki, a recognized scholar in the field. In his discussion of the role of nature in Zen, he says a number of significant things:

1. "Zen is right in the midst of the ocean of becoming. It shows no desire to escape from its tossing waves. It does not antagonize Nature; it does not treat Nature as if it were an enemy to be conquered, nor does it stand away from Nature. It is indeed Nature itself."[14]

2. "I am in Nature and Nature is in me. Not mere participation in each other, but a fundamental identity."[15]

3. "If you wish to seek the Buddha, you ought to see into your own Nature (*hsing*); for this Nature is the Buddha himself."[16]

4. "A *satori* event takes place . . . and there is for the first time a possibility of communication—a wonderful event, biologically speaking, in the evolution of consciousness, in which Nature comes to itself and becomes Man."[17]

5. "Nature is already Man, or otherwise no Man could come out of it. It is ourselves who fail to be conscious of the fact."[18]

---

14. Ibid., 255.
15. Ibid., 240.
16. Ibid., 87.
17. Ibid., 247.
18. Ibid., 248.

These statements don't really need any commentary. It is clear that Nature is the ultimate reality. In the experience of Satori, Nature becomes Man. In other words, Nature is potentially Man and becomes Man in the experience of Satori.

The second statement in our Zen model is that reality is something to be enjoyed and to be attuned to. Zen has its roots in the *Prajna-paramita sutras*. We have seen that early Buddhism considered this world as made up of dharmas—phenomenal realities that are valued negatively. These sutras considered these dharmas to be empty, lacking substance. Thus the concept of emptiness implied a very positive attitude toward nature and the secular world.

During the Southern Sung dynasty (1127–1279) Zen became the dominant form of Buddhism and the major spiritual influence on Chinese culture. The Sung master were known for being landscape painters with an emphasis on mountains, waters, mists, rocks, trees, and birds. This also showed the influence of Taoism.

The third statement in our model of Zen is that if one becomes responsive to one's inner nature, one then becomes attuned to reality as a whole. Life then becomes alive, spontaneous, free and in harmony with the whole—a spiritual hypothetical. "The whole system of Zen discipline," Suzuki says, "may [thus] be said to be nothing but a series of attempts to set us absolutely free from all forms of bondage."[19]

This freedom is portrayed as a manifestation of the Unconscious. The Unconscious is thus identified with "no-mind-ness." No-mind-ness is the Unconscious manifesting itself. This is the opposite of being deliberate and reflective about what one is doing.

This emphasis upon spontaneity is also found in Zen's view of archery and art. In its approach to archery the archer does not make the string taut, and then decide to release it. Rather, the string is made taut and then the arrow "shoots itself." This happens without the use of mind or choice. The release of the arrow just happens.

In a similar way with respect to the use of a brush for writing or painting, Watts tells us, "The brush must draw by itself. This cannot happen if one does not practice constantly. But neither can it happen if one makes an effort."[20]

---

19. Ibid., 162.
20. Watts, *Way*, 189.

This brings us to the fourth tenet—that life of the mind leads to spiritual death. Suzuki quotes an ancient Zen scholar as saying, "Deliberate thinking and discursive understanding amount to nothing; they belong to the household of ghosts; they are like a lamp in the broad daylight; nothing shines out of them."[21] It follows from this that one should not seek to attain enlightenment. Hui-chung, a disciple of Hui-neng, said the following: "When mind is not, who talks about attaining Buddhahood? To think that there is something called Buddhahood which is to be attained, this is cherishing the idea of a mind; to cherish the idea of a mind is an attempt to accomplish something that flows out; this being so, there is no no-mindness here."[22]

Enlightenment is the operation of the Unconscious and it is something that "flows." To introduce mind and deliberation in this context is to introduce demons and ghosts that produce mental constipation that brings bondage, destroys life, and results in spiritual death.

The fourth tenet of Zen is that one can become attuned to oneself and Nature by means of an abrupt experience referred to as satori. The Rinzai tradition regards an emphasis on meditation as an emphasis on achieving something, and to emphasize achieving something is to introduce mind, a form of constipation. Enlightenment, Satori, is thus something that happens; not something that is achieved.

## REPLY TO THE OBJECTIONS

Seeing Zen as historical phenomena requires seeing the influence of the *Prajna-paramita sutras* upon it and understanding these sutras requires seeing them as embodying a reaction to Theravada Buddhism. One cannot spell out the rejection of Theravada Buddhism without using language and pointing out similarities and differences. To see Zen from this perspective is to stand outside of it and do the kind of thing that our model for Zen attempts to do. Our model talks about values, spiritual hypotheticals, views of human nature, and a sixth category involving God, or the gods, Nirvana, and the Buddha Body. It applies these notions to particular historical contexts and sees religious traditions as working out interpretations of these elements in particular historical contexts.

21. Suzuki, *Zen*, 209.
22. Ibid., 203.

In the context of Zen, to keep to the strictures that the life of faith places on language would be to avoid doing history. Zen like any other religious phenomena is in part a historical phenomenon.

This analysis of the nature of religious views of life does not say that the practice of doing theology is importance. In the context of the early Rig Vedas theology was not practiced. There was, however, the belief in certain values, an assumption about human nature, and a view about the gods. That view of the gods was consistent with those values and that view of human nature. In Zen, theology is not practiced and the view is that it is harmful. However, it has values—freedom, spontaneity, and a very positive attitude about nature and life in the secular world. It also has a view of human nature according to which reason in the context of religion is harmful. Nature plays a role similar to the role that Brahman plays in the Upanishads.

What can be said about its spiritual hypotheticals? We know that attachment to language and theory is understood as destructive. We also know that the end is an experience of Satori. This is supposed to result in being attuned to one's inner self. Life is then supposed to become spontaneous and free. The goal here, it is said, requires working with a Zen master.

## A CRITICISM

In Zen a person's nature is part of the larger Nature. Life is supposed to be spontaneous and free involving the expressing of one's nature. In life, however, one person's freedom often leads to another person's suffering. This is evident in the case of the racist and the sexist. It is also true of life in general. One person's freedom is found in observing and appreciating a forest; another person's freedom is found in their work of cutting and harvesting that forest. In nature, the big fish expresses its nature by eating the little fish.

What the defender of Zen must assume is that the perfected saint is void of the sins that lead to conflict. There is no need for moral rules. In other words, besides a pessimistic view of our rational nature and our moral nature, Zen Buddhism assumes a romanticized view of Nature and our basic human nature.

To find a significant analogue to Zen in Western thought one should look to forms of nineteenth-century Romanticism. A website entitled *Henry David Thoreau Zen Sangha* mentions that this sangha meets every

Part 3 — Criticisms

Monday night in Newton at St. John's Episcopal Church.[23] Meetings always include Zen meditation (*zazen*) and Zen liturgy. A sangha is a Buddhist community, traditionally a community of monks.

---

23. http://newtonzen.org.

# PART 4

Theological Issues

# 12

# O. Hobart Mowrer

IN CHAPTER 3 A view of the nature of religious views of life was presented. It claimed that religious views of life involve beliefs and assumptions that fall into six categories, which are called the elements of religion. Chapters 4 through 9 showed that these categories apply to and help us understand early Hinduism, Buddhism, Judaism and Christianity. A response was then given to critics who claim that this analysis does not apply to Christianity because of the Christian view of Christ, chapter 10. A response was then given to those who claim that this analysis does not apply to Zen, chapter 11.

The role of the theologian is to assess religious views of life. This can best be done by assessing interpretations of the elements of religion. Thus far that role has been largely avoided. The purpose of this part of the book is not to develop a complete theology or to develop an interpretation of all of the elements. The purpose is to assess certain interpretations of certain elements. The method will be to try and figure out what we can learn from experience to properly assess various interpretations of the elements of religion.

Theories of counseling are sometimes linked to religious views of life. That is clearly the case with O. Hobart Mowrer and John Bradshaw. In this chapter we examine the views of Mowrer. This will include his criticisms of Calvin and his criticisms of Freud. Much of what Mowrer has to say involves a critique of these two individuals. Finally, a critique of the views of Mowrer will be given. The views defended here will then be used to critique Advaita Vedanta philosophy and early Buddhism.

The discussion of John Bradshaw will be put off until the next chapter.

# Part 4—Theological Issues

## INTRODUCTION

O. Hobart Mowrer (1907–1985) was research professor of psychology at the University of Illinois from 1948 until his retirement in 1975. In 1954 he was president of the American Psychological Association. He received his PhD at Johns Hopkins in 1932. He then taught and did research first at Yale, and then at Harvard. During the war he worked at the Office of Strategic Services.

When he was fourteen years old, after his father's death, he suffered from depression. This became a recurring problem. Even though he was a psychologist whose research was in learning theory, he also identified with Freud and went to a Freudian on several occasions to address the problem of depression. Sometimes this treatment had temporary benefits, but the problem kept recurring. This was at least one factor that led him to be critical of Freudian psychoanalytic theory.

While in the office of Strategic Services he was attracted to the views of Harry Stack Sullivan. Sullivan believed that disturbances in human relations with significant others can lead to unfortunate mental consequences. Mowrer became convinced that being deceptive with people you care much about is the primary source of neurosis. He then read some of the fictional and nonfictional works of Lloyd Douglas (1877–1951)—a writer who had been a Lutheran and then a Congregational minister.[1] He then joined a Presbyterian church.

He was not happy with the church. He thought that its liberalism led it to undermining the importance of sin and to identify with the views of Freud. His church was in the tradition of John Calvin. He was also very critical of Calvin.

In 1959 and 1960 articles about Mowrer appeared in *Newsweek*, *Time*, and the *American*. His views stirred interest among psychologists which led to a session where his views were discussed. What interested the national media was his claim that the word "sin" ought to be a part of the vocabulary of psychology.

One of his themes is that theology is often very much tied to the Middle Ages. Reformation theology made improvements, but it is still to a great extent tied to the Middle Ages. It needs to be reformed and brought into the modern world of science. It needs to take seriously what we can learn from

---

1. *The Robe*, *The Big Fisherman*, and *Magnificent Obsession* were some of his notable works.

sensory experience. There ought to be a harmony between psychopathology and theology. This author is sympathetic to that point of view.

## HUMAN NATURE

Mowrer begins his book *The Crisis in Psychiatry and Religion* by addressing the broad philosophical question of understanding ourselves as human beings. Much psychological thought, he says, has perceived the mind as an instrument to help the body survive. This has been influenced by Darwin. Mowrer does not doubt that much has been accomplished by this organic approach to the mind. The mind, he says, presumably evolved from the body, but having evolved it has its own special needs. The question Mowrer raises is this: Is there not a reciprocal way that the body serves the mind?

From a common sense point of view, can it not be said that this is what the practice of medicine is all about? When people go on diets and read about how to stay healthy, are they not using the mind to try to train the body? Mowrer seems to think that this kind of approach has not been recognized and emphasized enough in psychotherapy. This is what he calls the "old school" approach—one that has been assumed in theology.

Things, he says, are changing, however. Research has turned to problems such as interpersonal competence and to a study of group therapy—things that have been of interest to religious thinkers.

To the question of what we are as human beings, Mowrer says that we are not just bodies or organisms, but persons. We are persons who by nature are social creatures. We mature through the influence of other people; our lives are lived in relationships to other people. Personality, he says, "can be properly understood and appreciated only in terms of sociality, i.e., interpersonal and moral value systems."[2]

## MORAL VALUES, SIN, AND GUILT

If personality can only be understood in terms of moral value systems, then there is an important question that should be asked: How should we determine an appropriate moral value system? Mowrer does not raise that question, however.

2. Mowrer, *Crisis*, 44.

## Part 4—Theological Issues

He had a background of doing research in learning theory. He knew what empirical, scientific research is all about. He was also aware of the difference between what an empirical method can establish, and statements about what things are morally right, wrong, good, and bad. He did not doubt, however, that we could have knowledge of the latter. He is critical of those who deny this.

In approaching his discussion of sin he says, "We find that not only have we disavowed the connection between manifest misconduct and psychopathology; we have, also, very largely abandoned belief in right and wrong, virtue and sin, in general."[3] A little bit later he goes on to say, "We have the spectacle of grown men and women soberly insisting that, in effect, they cannot tell right from wrong—and that no one else can."[4]

Who is he referring to? In the first sentence he is referring to himself and his audience, but does not intend to be taken literally. He has not abandoned the belief in right and wrong. In the second quote he is referring to "those misguided persons." He is attacking either moral skepticism which says that we cannot know anything about what is moral; or he is attacking moral nihilism which says there is no such thing as something which is morally right and wrong, good and bad. We found the latter in Zen. These two quotes are from a chapter which was a paper given to the American Psychological Association. The "we" he is referring to is thus to a great extent members of the American Psychological Association. In 1954 he was president of that association. He should thus know something about them.

Both problems are philosophical problems. The way to address these problems, I believe, is to indicate that the skeptic and the nihilist make judgments, at times, about how certain people have mistreated others. It might be about the very rich, about those on Wall Street or the one percent; it might be about how they, out of self-interest, have ruined the lives of others. Or it might be about those at the bottom of society who want to live off the gratuity of government and not be responsible for their actions. Such judgments are moral judgments.

What a skeptic and nihilist should do is try to be consistent about such judgments and reflect on how they should be made. In other words, the person should take a moral point of view since he or she makes moral judgments. To do otherwise runs the danger of being inconsistent and irrational.

3. Ibid., 41.
4. Ibid.

## O. Hobart Mowrer

Contrary to what was just said, Mowrer says that one cannot deal with a moral nihilist in a rational, logical way. He then gives an argument for morality. He says that a social order requires a moral order. "I know not a single reputable sociologist or anthropologist who would seriously maintain that we can have a society which does not internalize, as they would say, the norms of the culture. Otherwise, we have not a society."[5]

In other words, he has a pragmatic argument for morality. Morality is built into the nature of what we are as human beings and a society requires it. Note that this pragmatic argument does not yield by itself a moral perspective that can be considered justified. The necessity of a moral value system does not require a justifiable moral value system.

To find a justifiable one would require considering moral values systems that people have accepted and have defended. In that context one can take a particular moral point of view and defend it as superior. In this way a justifiable moral point of view is possible. It is not my role and function in this book to do that.

When Mowrer introduces the subject of sin he raises the following question: Is "real guilt or sin . . . relevant to the problem of psychopathology and psychotherapy?"[6] His answer, of course, is "yes." The problem is that the claim that something is a real guilt needs real reasons and justification.

The other question here is the question of why he uses the word "sin." Mowrer justifies his use of the word "sin" by the fact that it is a strong word. Its strength, he says, is an asset, not a liability. "Immoral," and "morally wrong," he says won't do.[7] Why does being really, really morally wrong justify introducing the word "sin"? This word is understood as a part of certain religious traditions—Judaism, Islam, and Christianity. It was a surprise to the press and to many that he uses it and thinks that it is proper to use it in the discipline of psychology. It is alright to use a word in an unusual way as long as one makes clear what one is doing and why. He often does not do that. He says that he is using it instead of "immoral," and "morally wrong." He justifies his use of it by just saying that he is using it because of its strength. What he should say is that he means morally wrong, but he is using the word "sin" instead because of its strength. In other words, he is not using it in a religious sense. That would make things clearer.

---

5. Ibid., 162.
6. Ibid., 45.
7. Ibid., 42.

Mowrer has three basic concerns which he expresses in three statements:

1. "Personality disorder of sufficient severity to require hospitalization is today commonly acknowledged as the nation's number-one 'health problem.'"[8]

2. "Protestantism has handled the problem of personal guilt very poorly."[9]

3. Why has it handled guilt so poorly? "The only way this present writer can understand the situation is . . . in terms of the absurdity of the Reformation doctrine of human guilt and divine grace."[10]

## MOWRER'S CRITIQUE OF PAUL

Above Mowrer refers to the Reformation. He often mentions Calvin, but never quotes Calvin nor refers to what Calvin said. He says that his primary concern is how Calvin and the Reformation have influenced modern culture. The person he discusses is Paul. We might say that what concerns Mowrer is how Paul-Luther-Calvin and the Reformation have influenced modern culture. In critiquing that point of view he discusses Paul. Calvin and Luther based their views on Paul.

Mowrer summarizes the views of Paul by quoting Romans 3:24–26: "They [people] are justified by his grace as a gift, through the redemption which is in Christ Jesus, whom God put forward as expiation by his blood, to be received by faith."

We saw in chapter 8 that for Paul faith and works are incompatible. An emphasis on works brings spiritual death. Justification before God is based on faith apart from works. Mowrer rejects that point of view and quotes from the Epistle of James to support his point of view:

> What does it profit, my brethren, if a man says he has faith but has not works? Can faith save him? If a brother or sister is ill clad and in lack of daily food, and one of you say to them, "Go in peace, be warmed and filled," without giving them the things needed for the body, what does it profit? So faith by itself, if it has no works, is dead . . . Show me your faith apart from your works, and I by my works will show you my faith. (Jas 2:14–18)

8. Ibid., 157.
9. Ibid.
10. Ibid., 175.

This seems to be a direct attack on the views of Paul. That it is such an attack is reinforced by the fact that James also attacks Paul's interpretation of Abraham, Paul's hero. James says,

> Do you want to be shown, you foolish fellow, that faith apart from works is barren? Was not Abraham our father justified by works, when he offered his son Isaac upon the altar? You see that faith was active along with his works, and faith was completed by works, and the scripture was fulfilled, which says, "Abraham believed God, and it was reckoned to him as righteousness"; and he was called the friend of God. You see that a man is justified by works and not by faith alone. (Jas 2:20–24)

## THE AUTHORSHIP OF JAMES

Is the author here the brother of Jesus? If it were, it would carry significant weight. The brother of Jesus was named James, and referred to as "James, the Just." Marcus Borg does not think that it was written by the brother of Jesus because the author's Greek language was too sophisticated to be the brother of Jesus. Besides, he does not refer to himself as the brother but this way: "James, a servant of God and of the Lord Jesus Christ" (Jas 1:1).

Reza Aslan is the author of the popular book *Zealot: The Life and Times of Jesus of Nazareth*. In it he notes that it was a common practice to name a book after someone as a way of honoring that person and reflecting that person's point of view. He says that this is true of the gospels of Mark, Matthew, and John, as well as Colossians, Ephesians, 2 Thessalonians, 1 and 2 Timothy, and Titus.[11]

His claim is that there are reasons to think that James was written by someone representing the brother of Jesus. Twice in Acts Paul is described as coming before James and the elders of the church in Jerusalem. Acts 21:20–21 has these leaders say, "You see, brother, how many thousands there are among the Jews of those who have believed; they are zealous for the law, and they have been told about you that you teach all the Jew who among the Gentiles to forsake Moses, telling them not to circumcise their children and observe the customs."

The background of this event is that Paul had previously been before a counsel which included James, the apostles, and elders (Acts 15). His views

---

11. Aslan, *Zealot*, 204.

about the law and circumcision were debated. James then laid down a ruling which might be called a middle-of-the-road ruling. The Greeks in his churches did not have to be circumcised, but they were to refrain from what was sacrificed to idols, from blood, from what is strangled, and from unchastity (Acts 15:28).

Paul, however, in his letters shows disdain for James and the leaders in the Jerusalem church. In Galatians 2:5–6 he dismisses them saying that by those who reputed to be something meant nothing to him. Second Corinthians 11:13–23 says of these leaders,

> For such men are false apostles, deceitful workmen, disguising themselves as apostles of Christ . . . Are they Hebrews? So am I. Are they Israelites? So am I. Are they descendants of Abraham? So am I. Are they servants of Christ? I am a better one—I am talking like a madman—with far better labors, far more imprisonments, with countless beatings, and often near death.

According to the *Antiquities* of Josephus, "James, the brother of Jesus, the one they call the messiah," was charged by a high priest with blasphemy and not keeping the law. He was then sentenced to be stoned to death.[12] This was 62 CE. The believers in Jerusalem were of course outraged by this and continued to have fondness for he who was their leader and the brother of Jesus.

Given this sharp conflict and the influence that Paul had on so many churches, one should expect that after the death of James someone would write a manuscript representing the views of James, their beloved leader.

## MOWRER'S CRITIQUE OF THE REFORMATION

Mowrer quotes James to counter what Paul says in Romans. Mowrer's main reason for rejecting the views of Paul, however, is to first note that the views of the Reformation are based on Paul. He then argues that the Reformation has handled the problem of guilt badly. He gives three reasons for this: (1) Believing in Christ does not address the real guilt that people experience. (2) Paul's view of human nature makes things worse. (3) Paul's view of the cross makes no sense.

Normally people believe themselves guilty at times for things they do or didn't do. Mowrer says that it is a sign of character. A psychopath does

---

12. Ibid., 199.

not experience guilt. According to Mowrer, for a Christian to dismiss every experience of guilt because he or she is a believer does not address the psychological problem. If a husband does something to hurt his wife, it makes no sense to think of the cross and to think therefore one is forgiven. It is his responsibility to address the wife: to express sorrow, to ask for forgiveness, and to do what he can to address whatever harm has been done.

Second, Mowrer says that Paul's view of human nature has made the problem of guilt worse and makes no sense. He says,

> While holding that when we behave badly it is by our own volition and choice, it then insists, paradoxically, that when we behave well this is by the grace of God, for which we deserve no credit. In other words, the doctrine is that when we are confronted by an apparent option of good and evil, we can choose only the evil, and are fully accountable for having done so, but if we do the good rather than the evil, this is because of God's will and direction. In short, man can willfully and deliberately act himself into a state of perdition; but he cannot, by the reverse strategy, save or redeem himself. Salvation comes, if it comes at all, only by the grace and unpredictable favor of God.[13]

This latter statement refers, of course, to Paul's view of election. There are two things to note about this passage. There is nothing logically inconsistent in the view that Mowrer is objecting to. He thinks that it is obviously wrong-headed, but not all will agree. Second, we saw in our discussion of Paul in chapter 8 that Marcus Borg would not agree with this interpretation of Paul. He interprets Paul as saying that salvation is the transformation of human lives. If there is nothing good that human beings can do, then life cannot be transformed. We will come to this issue later.

What Mowrer says is that Paul's view of the fundamental sinfulness of human nature and our inability to do anything about it leads to despair and uncertainty. He says that it is this kind of uncertainty and despair expressed in Soren Kierkegaard's *Sickness unto Death* and *Attack upon Christianity*.[14] By emphasizing sin and guilt, and not providing the tools to address the problem, he said that the Reformation provided the need for psychotherapy. Freud then conveniently stepped in to fill the need. The problem, he said, is that Freud did not provide the cure.

---

13. Mowrer, *Crises*, 159.
14. Ibid., 160.

The third reason Mowrer gives for the Reformation not handling the problem of guilt properly is Paul's view of the cross. For Paul, Mowrer says, if one believes then the problem of guilt has been solved. Christ has paid for our sins on the cross. Whereas Paul's view of human nature says that we cannot do anything to help ourselves, his view of the cross says that we do need to do anything. It has been done for us.

When Paul says, "We are justified by his blood" (Rom 5:9), Mowrer understands Paul to be assuming the substitutionary theory of atonement. He does not explain what that is, but refers to it as a piece of nonsense. To shed some light on the problem it would help to say something about the logic of the cross.

We have seen that the Yahwist recognized sacrifices, but their importance was not stressed. Over time they became more important. In the last source of the Torah, the Priestly source, religion was centered in the priests and their sacrifices. At times when sacrifices are practiced they can be considered as tokens, as signs of thanksgiving or of repentance for sin. In a similar way, most Protestants consider the elements in the Lord's Supper as tokens. A conservative, however, will regard a sacrifice as a way to get something from God that the person wants, or a way to make up for sin that has been committed. When Paul says, "We are justified by his blood" (Rom 5:9), he is taking the conservative view.

One of Mowrer's interesting criticisms of theology is that it tends to be metaphysical and abstract, not linked to people's experiences. It is often, he says, "undisciplined verbiage."[15] He asks, "By what operations is it validated, tested, refined, and clarified?"[16] The criticism of being metaphysical and not linked to people's experience can also be said of religion at times. Using tokens to express thanks or remorse are appropriate. To use sacrifices to affect God's actions and behavior is a different kind of thing, a metaphysical thing that has no justification in experience. Paul is in that tradition when he speaks of being justified by the blood of Jesus. In a liberal orientation, a sacrifice could be a token which represents remorse. For Paul it is not remorse or repentance which is important. It is the shedding of blood and faith.

In chapter 8 we saw that for Paul faith involved trust, loyalty, or commitment. Mowrer, however, considers faith to be belief. In chapter 8 we saw that for Paul faith usually involved trust or commitment. Genesis tells us

15. Ibid., 171.
16. Ibid.

that Abraham trusted God and Abraham was reckoned righteous for this. Note that this reckoning is a de jure kind of thing, a legal type of affair. Paul then says that what applies to Abraham applies to the person who believes God raised Jesus from the dead. In both cases being reckoned as righteous is a de jure type of affair. It does not involve the transformation of human lives or repentance. Paul's speaking of being justified by the cross and by blood makes this clear. Thus whether faith is believing, trusting, or a commitment, it doesn't make any difference. Justification is still a legal, de jure type of affair. It is not linked to repentance or a change in one's form of life.

Those who identify with Paul have developed various theories of atonement to figure out why the cross of Jesus is important. All of these theories assume that Paul's view is the proper one. Mowrer is not in that tradition and responds by quoting James.

Mowrer assumes that Paul believes in the substitutionary theory of the atonement. Question: What is the substitutionary theory of atonement? The view is that Christ's death was a terrible suffering death by the choice of an innocent, sinless person. According to this theory the death of Jesus functions as a substitute for the suffering death we deserve.

A response to this is this: If I deserve to be in jail for a month, it makes no sense to say that someone else could serve the time in jail that I deserve. It would not be the punishment that I deserve.

Earlier we quoted Mowrer as saying, "Personality disorder of sufficient severity to require hospitalization is today commonly acknowledged as the nation's number-one 'health-problem.'"[17] His explanation for that is that the Reformation has shaped modern society in such a way that the problem of guilt has not been addressed. It is thus not the proper interpretation of Paul that is important. What is important is how modern society has been affected by the Reformation. Mowrer says that the modern society has gained from the Reformation the belief that people are too corrupt and sinful to do anything about the problem of guilt and salvation. The Reformation says, however, that God has provided an answer by means of the cross. All that one has to do is believe or have faith. Faith apart from works linked to the cross is the answer. For Mowrer the problem of this approach lies in its view of human nature; its identification with faith apart from works, and its view of the cross.

What is Mowrer's alternative?

---

17. Ibid., 157.

## Part 4—Theological Issues

### MOWRER ON GUILT

Mowrer talks about real guilt. I am going to talk about the experience of guilt because talk of real guilt involves complications. Besides it is possible that a person could be really guilty without feeling guilty or considering himself or herself to be guilty. Psychopaths fall into this category.

According to Mowrer the experience of guilt is a sign of character. A person condemns himself or herself. A psychopath does not experience guilt because of a lack of character. The experience itself can be very painful, depending upon how awful the deed is considered.

Mowrer suggests a case where a person feels real guilty because of something he did. If a minister were to say to him, "No problem; Christ died for your sins on the cross," Mowrer says that this would not likely address the problem. That would not likely alleviate the guilt he feels, or it could just lead to the feeling of guilt being sublimated. If other people accept him, that is not going to address his problem. His problem is with his conscience which condemns his action. He has to come to accept himself.

At this point Mowrer looks at the policy of the Catholic Church. He quotes the Lutheran theologian Jaroslav Pelikan who thinks that Protestants are missing something valuable. Pelikan says, "Through the administration of these three steps—contrition, confession, and satisfaction—the church has a splendid opportunity to apply the healing power of the gospel to the concrete needs of the penitent."[18] Rather than speak of penance, Mowrer speaks of changing one's practices and, when possible, restoring what harm has been done—restitution.

### Confession

When a person causes a significant harm or a significant wrong, but does not admit it, then the person hides what was done. This hiding causes significant psychological strain and isolates the individual from others.

A person, Mowrer says, "is preeminently a social creature and that he lives or dies, psychologically and personally as a function of the openness, community, relatedness, and integrity which by good actions he attains and by evil actions destroys."[19] People who have good relationships, significant ties, and good interactions with other people will normally be mentally

---

18. Ibid., 191.
19. Ibid., 44.

healthy. What he has in mind are "relatives, friends, colleagues, neighbors. Here is where the real 'break through' to community and personal authenticity comes."[20] The problem is that the sense of guilt often severs or strains these relationships.

At this point Mowrer turns to Dietrich Bonhoeffer for support. He refers to a passage in Bonhoeffer's book *Life Together* where he quotes James 5:16, "Confess your faults one to another." Bonhoeffer then says,

> He who is alone with his sin is strictly alone . . . In confession the break thorough to community takes place. Sin demands to have a man by himself. It withdraws him from the community . . . The more isolated the more a person is, the more destructive will be the power of sin over him, and the more deeply he becomes involved in it, the more disastrous is his isolation . . . In confession the light of the Gospel breaks into the darkness and seclusion of the heart . . . The unexpressed must by openly spoken and acknowledged . . . It is a hard struggle until the sin is openly admitted. But God breaks gates of brass and iron.[21]

Note that Bonhoeffer is quoting James. As mentioned above, James agrees with Mowrer not only on the importance of works—as opposed to faith alone, but also on the importance of confession.

The way Mowrer and Bonhoeffer understand confession, contrition is part of the confession. A person who confesses recognizes that he or she has done a wrong. In the confession the person expresses sorrow for having done the wrong.

## Restitution

Consider the following case: Let us suppose that John and Mary are good friends. If John significantly hurts Mary, this will produce a wound in their relationship. For Mowrer, John's well-being and our well-being are tied to healthy relationships with one another. If Mary forgives John because he is a nice guy, this will not address his own sense of guilt for having hurt her. Nor will John's saying "I'm sorry" adequately address the problem. Mowrer says that John needs to do something to address the wound itself, to heal it. There should be a program to address the harm that has been done. He notes that some churches are coming to see the importance of confession.

20. Ibid., 180.
21. Ibid., 191.

This, he says, is good. What they ought to do, however, is emphasize restitution and reformation.[22] Confession, repentance, and a program of restitution and reformation should be a policy.

Mowrer is impressed by both the Salvation Army and Alcoholics Anonymous who follow these procedures. He is impressed with their effectiveness. He says, "There is no clear evidence of the efficacy of professional psychotherapy—certainly nothing to compare with the manifest transformations achieved by AA and the Salvation Army."[23] In fact, he suggests AA as a model. He says,

> No other therapeutic or "redemptive" movement, within the church or without, has in recent times been so successful as Alcoholics Anonymous. Here guilt is seen as basic and real; and its open admission is regarded as an indispensable first step, to be followed by a definite program of good works and restitution.[24]

## MOWRER'S CRITIQUE OF FREUD

To understand Mowrer it is important to understand his critique of Freud. As mentioned above, Mowrer accepted Freud's view of therapy for a long time and underwent therapy in several periods in his life—sometimes extensively. The problem was that it didn't work.

According to Freud problems such as depression and psychosis are caused by the super-ego repressing sexual urges, the id. This is the way Mowrer describes it:

> Freud held that, as a result of a too intensive socialization, some individuals develop so great a fear of their sexual and hostile feelings that, eventually, they even deny these feelings access to consciousness and that it is the alarm which the ego feels when these impulses clamor for recognition and expression (i.e., the danger, as Freud called it, of the "return of the repressed") that generates the characteristic neurotic effects of depression, anxiety, and panic. In 1950 the present writer . . . hypothesized that in neurosis it is actually the individual's *conscience* that has been repudiated and

---

22. Ibid., 196.
23. Ibid., 140.
24. Ibid., 109.

"repressed" rather than his "instincts," thus shifting the emphasis from Freud's *impulse* theory of neurosis to a *guilt* theory.[25]

From Mower's point of view, Freud considered the superego, conscience, as irrational, too oppressive. Mowrer said that it is a good thing to refrain our impulses. It prevents other people from getting hurt. From Freud's point of view the superego needs to be restrained. The id, human's sexual impulses, needs to be permitted to find a way to express itself. We need more self-love. Restraints should be placed on that irrational boss, the superego, which seeks to control our natural inclinations.

Mowrer has two arguments against Freud. First, Freudian analysis, he says, doesn't work. He does not refer to his own experiences, but quotes Dr. H. J. Eysenck. He was Director of the Psychological Laboratories of the Institute of Psychiatry at the University of London. He says, "The success of the Freudian revolution seemed complete. Only one thing went wrong: *the patients did not get any better.*"[26] Mowrer says that among psychoanalysts there is a common understanding that people don't get cured. Mowrer contrasts this with the significant success that has been found in AA and in the Salvation Army.

Mowrer's other argument concerns those who are classified as schizophrenic. According to Freud such individuals should be far above normal in their conduct because they have internalized the norms of the society. They have repressed instincts that are contrary to their conscience and these norms. He says, however, that the evidence points to just the opposite being the case. He cites, for example, a study by Hock and Polatin who did a study of a large number of borderline schizophrenics and reported the following:

> In all the writers' cases, they observed that the patient usually told of a great many sexual preoccupations showing autoerotic, oral, anal, homosexual and heterosexual tendencies, and ideas which sometimes resembled a textbook of *psychopathia sexualis*. These polymorphous perverse manifestations, this chaotic organization of the patient's sexuality is rather characteristic of these schizophrenic cases.[27]

---

25. Ibid., 83–84.
26. Ibid., 133.
27. Ibid., 90.

Mowrer points out that for both Calvin and Freud our fate is a product of circumstances for which we are not responsible. We are helpless to do anything about it.[28] Calvin talked about predestination; Freud about psychic determinism. For Calvin we have a sinful nature built into us. For Freud our social environment instills in us an oppressive superego. Here we have two views of human nature, element three. He rejected both.

For Mowrer guilt can be addressed and resolved by the means of confession, repentance, and reformation. Here we have a spiritual hypothetical. This requires a person assuming responsibility and taking steps of doing something about it. Here we have an alternative view of human nature.

## A CRITIQUE OF MOWRER

The critique of Mowrer is going to be based on three questions: Is conscience always rational? Is a person's love of self always adequate? And, what constitutes real guilt?

### Is Conscience Always Rational?

One of Mowrer's main points is that guilt is something that people hide. This hiding, he says, takes psychological energy, causes anxiety, and sometimes leads to neurosis or psychosis. Conscience and people's sense of guilt are good things because conscience functions as a policeman that checks people's behavior and leads to everyone's good. According to Freud conscience tends to be irrational, too overbearing and often needs to be moderated for our own good. An important issue here is the extent to which Freud is right. In his more cautious moments Mowrer will grant that conscience can be irrational and overbearing, but he never discusses these kinds of cases. He often speaks as if all forms of neurosis were rooted in rational guilt.

In this area John Calvin was influenced by both Paul and Martin Luther. Both Paul and Luther were religious perfectionists whose perfectionism led to their spiritual destruction. Paul is clear on this point. He says that when the law came, "I died." Paul referred to himself as having been an ideal Pharisee. Pharisees were known for their rigorous interpretation and application of the law. Luther's spiritual advisor told him that he took religion too seriously. Perfectionism can cause spiritual death. Ideals are

28. Ibid., 159–63.

internalized which eventually they cannot live up to. This leads to a sense of guilt and spiritual death. To say that conscience was their downfall may mislead because it was their religious ideals more than moral beliefs that debilitated them.

Are there ideals today that have a similar debilitating affect? I once had a discussion with a drug counselor who we will call Carol. She had an interesting story to tell with respect to her own experience with drugs. She grew up in a middle class family in which her father was a very talented successful person. He was very successful in school and as a musician, sportsman, and business person. He also achieved significant stature in his community. As she grew she was in awe of him and internalized his ideals. The problem was that she was a flop in many of the things where her father had been successful. She was a terrible musician and could not excel in school. She came to despise herself for her inability to live up to those ideals that had become a part of her. The pain from this self-contempt led to drugs and to finding ego fulfillment among peers who were into drugs.

Mowrer says that every society will have some kind of moral principles that members internalize. Does not every culture and religious community recognize certain ideals that tend to shape the lives of children? Mowrer is right in saying that moral principles are important to a society, but it is also true that we want good scientists, artists, teachers, ministers, business leaders, doctors, and athletes. Because of this, it is always possible for children to internalize forms of perfection that they cannot live up to and to have an experience such as Carol had, and Luther and Paul had. A religious community ought to be graded in part by the values and ideals it recognizes and embodies—element one. But herein lays a potential problem because a religious community should also be the source of life—element two. There is always the danger of the ideals within the community leading to experiences of spiritual death as happened to Paul, Luther, and Carol.

## Is a Person's Self-Love Always Adequate?

A related issue is the relative importance of self-love and self-respect which Freudians emphasize. Mowrer criticizes Freud for failing to recognize that self-contempt arising out of guilt can be a good thing. Conscience is a policeman and everyone benefits from the presence of officers representing the law. If we agree with Mowrer that experiences of guilt can be a good thing, which I think we should, there is still the broader question of whether people sometimes have a lack of self-respect and self-love. That is the view of Bradshaw. He will be discussed in the next chapter.

Let me suggest two important dictums: "A person's well-being is tied to a person's sense of self-worth" and "a positive sense of self-worth arises out of having been shown love and respect."

Children who have never been shown love and respect have difficulty feeling good about themselves. When an environment tells a child that he or she does not count for anything, then the child is likely to internalize what the environment teaches and have a sense of self-contempt. This is likely to produce a sense of pain. It is also likely to lead to antisocial behavior to gain recognition for oneself in order to ease the pain.

What is true of children is sometimes true of adults. This author has spent a significant amount of time in a dementia unit of a nursing home. In that context the environment sometimes sends a message that a resident counts for nothing. This sense of counting for nothing is then sometimes internalized and leads to a sense of self-contempt. From this comes pain and often antisocial behavior to gain recognition and ease the pain. The response of the nursing home is often to find some kind of drug to retard the antisocial behavior.

To have a proper respect for oneself, to have a good self-image, is to think of oneself as having intrinsic worth, as being important in and of oneself. This is analogous to Kant's principle that a person should always be treated as an end and never as a means only. This can also be considered from the perspective of moral values, i.e., persons ought to be valued as something important in and of themselves. The argument here is that it is relevant to spiritual hypotheticals. A person's own well-being requires respect for oneself; this in turn requires being shown love and respect.

This is an emphasis that Mowrer fails to develop.

## What Constitutes Real Guilt?

In the beginning of this chapter I discussed the problem of real guilt. Rather than summarize what has been said there, I am going to tell a story that indicates the problem.

I once had a conversation with a nurse, call her Mary, who is a supervisor in a nursing home. She talked about her work and the problems she faced. She then mentioned a case in which there was a problem of guilt.

In this case an elderly person was pushed by her physician into an unexpected amputation of a limb. Her children then put her into a nursing home believing that the amputation made this necessary. The mother was upset because she was not prepared psychologically for either the amputation or the nursing home. The children felt frustrated and concerned. One of the daughters then became hypercritical of the management of the nursing home and its staff. When the family was brought together for a discussion, the hypercritical daughter broke down and wept. She realized at that point that her own sense of guilt was the reason for the attack on the nursing home.

This case is interesting for a couple of reasons. For one thing, it gives evidence that a sense of guilt can have a debilitating effect on people's lives. It can lead to neurotic behavior. It is also interesting because it relates to the question of what constitutes real guilt. Not everyone in this family felt guilty about putting their mother in this home. Whether the one daughter who felt guilty was really guilty is a difficult problem. Real guilt requires acts that are really wrong.

What seems to be important is to have counselors/therapists/ministers that are morally sensitive and can talk and reflect with people about relevant moral issues. This is a perspective emphasized by John Dienhart in his book *A Cognitive Approach to the Ethics of Counseling Psychology*. Dienhart points out that getting a person to reflect in a moral way about a situation is not the same as indoctrination. For one thing it need not be, and normally should not be, a matter of getting the person to take a particular course of action. Besides, an honest taking into consideration of the various reasons for acting in different ways is what rational inquiry is all about. It involves a taking into consideration the consequences of various actions. The goal is to help a person make up his or her mind about what is morally proper in a particular situation.

Dienhart faults Freudians and behaviorists for not having any kind of rational view of the nature of moral development. From that perspective a person's moral perspective has its roots only in the authority of the family or the society. It cannot have any kind of rational basis.

Dienhart defends a reworked version of Lawrence Kohlberg's theory of moral development. This theory was introduced in chapter 3. Its most recent version is found in chapter 3 of Kohlberg's *The Psychology of Moral Development*, volume 2. He is a cognitive psychologist who is credited with having created a new field within psychology—moral development. He seeks to give an analysis of the stages of moral development—stages that can be found across cultural lines. He does an empirical study of moral development. In this analysis the level of moral development is determined by the kinds of reasons a child will give for moral behavior. At the lowest level children consider right to be what avoids punishment. He then seeks to show that there are levels of development in a child's moral maturation that are not determined by culture.

## CRITIQUE: ADVAITA VEDANTA AND EARLY BUDDHISM

In the discussion above it was said that self-love is important. Without it people will feel pain and are likely to act in abnormal ways to get attention; to get what they lack. This is not unusual in children and in elderly adults. For both groups it is easy for people to ignore them and to not pay attention to them. They grasp after love and need love for their well-being.

There are religious perspectives that have denied that a person as a finite being should be regarded as important and as having significant worth. In Shankara's interpretation of the Upanishads, called Advaita Vedanta, the finite self, called jiva, is illusory, something not truly real. It should not be valued as something that is truly real. He takes seriously the Chandogya Upanishad which says, "There is no joy in the finite, only in the Infinite" (7:16–25). The spiritual hypothetical here is that real joy requires disvaluing the finite and valuing only the infinite. Besides, what is truly real is the infinite Brahman/Atman.

Let's recall the views of early Buddhism. Life is permeated by dukkha, which is sorrow and suffering. The cause of this suffering is tanha which is craving, a thirst for pleasure, for existence, for anything. The goal of the Noble Eightfold Path is to eliminate tanha, craving. When tanha ends, suffering ends, and we have non-attachment, dispassion, and renunciation.

The view defended in this chapter is that craving for love and respect is not a bad thing. It is part of human nature to crave for love and respect. People also have the need to love and respect themselves. They come to love and respect themselves by being shown love and respect. It is important to a person's well-being that love and respect be shown.

We have been discussing what Mowrer calls personal sins, and personal redemption designed to address the problems related to those sins. Mowrer also talks about corporate evil. There are forms of evil that apply to society as a whole and institutions within it. Correspondingly, there are spiritual hypotheticals that apply to society as a whole.

Before discussing them, however, the views of John Bradshaw will be presented and critiqued in chapter 13. He, like Mowrer, has a view of therapy which he integrates into a religious point of view. He differs significantly from Mowrer's point of view.

We will conclude with a discussion of corporate evil in chapters 14 and 15.

# 13

# John Bradshaw

IN CHAPTER 12 WE saw that O. Hobart Mowrer had a view of counseling which he integrates with a religious view of life. In this chapter we will see how Bradshaw does the same thing. The views of Bradshaw will then be compared with the views of Freud and Mowrer, and then critiqued.

Bradshaw is a counselor who did a televised series on the Public Broadcast System entitled "Bradshaw On: The Family." He is like Mowrer in that he is a religious person interested in therapy groups and wishes to integrate a view of therapy into a religious view of life. He also refers to himself as a theologian. He wrote a book in 1988 based on that PBS series with the same title. All quotations of Bradshaw and references to him will be taken from this book.

## INTRODUCTION

The book begins with a parable about Hugh. Hugh was a royal person, precious, unrepeatable, a trillion-dollar diamond in the rough. Here's the story:

> For the first 15 months of life, Hugh only knew himself from the reflections he saw in the eyes of his caretakers. Hugh was terribly unfortunate. His caretakers, although not blind, had glasses over their eyes. Each set of glasses already had an image on it so that each caretaker only saw Hugh according to the image on his glasses. Thus, even though Hugh's caretakers were physically present, not one of them ever actually saw him. By the time Hugh was

grown he was a mosaic of other people's images of him, none of which was who he really was. No one had really ever seen him, so no one had ever mirrored back to him what he really looked like. Consequently, Hugh thought he was the mosaic of images. He really did not know who he was. Sometimes in the dark of the night when he was alone, Hugh knew that something of profound importance was missing. He experienced that as a gnawing sense of emptiness—a deep void. Hugh tried to fill the emptiness and void with many things: power, worldly fame, money, possessions, chemical highs, food, sex, excitement . . . But no matter what he did, he never felt the gnawing emptiness go away . . . But alas! Hugh . . . went to his death never knowing who he was![1]

I have a confession to make. I have difficulty understanding this parable. It is supposed to shed light on our life situation. There is supposed to be a sense in which we at times have conflicting views of what we are and do not know who we are.

## CRITICISM ONE

Let me respond to this by saying something about what we are as human beings. Views here belong to the third of the elements of life. I suggest that we are the embodiment of a set of abilities, beliefs, assumptions, attitudes, dispositions and feelings. These "things" change over time. As we grow up they mature and develop and then eventually decline when we get older.

What do we know about ourselves? We know our bodies, and we have a fairly good idea of our abilities, beliefs, attitudes, dispositions and feelings. Sometimes we miscalculate our abilities, and of course we often don't know much about our relatives. In this story Hugh doesn't know who his parents were and did not know that he had royal lineage. That clearly is not the point of the story, however. There is supposed to be some deeper truth about who we are. Mowrer mentions that in counseling sometimes the question "who am I" is taken seriously. His response is that it is a piece of nonsense. Of course, he says, we know who we are.[2]

This parable is the beginning of this book. We should leave open the question of who Bradshaw thinks we are until we look into the book and see what it has to say. Maybe the book can give us something to learn.

1. Bradshaw, *On the Family*, x.
2. Mowrer, *Crisis*, 178–80.

Here are some important quotes from his first chapter:

> We now understand that families are dynamic social systems, having structural laws, components and rules. The most important rules are the rules that determine what it means to be a human being . . . Parenting forms children's core belief about themselves . . . The rules about raising children are the most sacred of all rules . . . [There exists] a cultural no talk rule. This "no talk" rule is rooted in the rules which govern parenting. Children are told to speak when spoken to; children are to be seen and not heard; children are to obey and to obey all adults [any adult] without question. To question is an act of disobedience. And so the rules are carried by the obedient child in all the adults who are raising families. The hidden child in every adult continues to obey so that the rules are carried multi-generationally.[3]

## CRITICISM TWO

Let us put what is said here in its historical context. This book was written in 1988. It is based on a series of programs presented earlier on PBS. In 1946, Dr. Benjamin Spock wrote his book *The Common Sense Book of Baby and Child Care*. It became a bestseller. Eventually it was translated into thirty-nine languages and over fifty million copies were sold. At the heart of his perspective was the view that a child is to be treated with respect and the unique qualities of each child are to be recognized and considered. These are the precisely the kinds of things Bradshaw emphasizes. Conservatives sometimes regard the failures of modern society to the influence of Spock's teaching. He was and is sometimes called the father of permissiveness—a criticism that he rejected. In this context to say that there is one set of rules for the family in our culture—rules that are autocratic and authoritarian—is inappropriate. It fails to recognize what might be called the Spock revolution. It fails to recognize the multiplicity of rules parents have.

## CRITICISM THREE

To understand Bradshaw we need to understand what he had in mind when he said that Hugh died without knowing who he was. He has two answers. One answer involves understanding the nature of shame and the

3. Bradshaw, *On the Family*, 4.

role it plays in our lives. He quotes Gershen Kaufman as saying that shame is "a sickness of the soul. It is the poignant experience of the self by the self . . . [It] is a wound felt from inside, dividing us both from ourselves and from one another."[4] Note the phrase "dividing us . . . from ourselves." A basic thesis of Bradshaw is that autocratic, authoritarian rules imbedded in the family breeds shame and produces this division.

Bradshaw seems to link all of the psychological ailments that people have to this shame. The list: "depression, alienation, self-doubt, isolating loneliness, paranoid and schizoid phenomena, compulsive disorders, splitting of the self, perfectionism, a deep sense of inferiority, inadequacy or failure, the so called borderline conditions and disorders of narcissism."[5] Whereas Mowrer emphasizes guilt almost exclusively, Bradshaw emphasizes shame exclusively.

In order to understand Bradshaw's view of the role of shame it is best to quote him at length: "To be safe and survive," he says, "a child must idealize his parent and make himself bad."[6] He then proceeds to explain this:

> If the child got shamed for feeling angry, sad or sexual, he will shame himself each time he feels angry, sad or sexual. All of his feelings, needs and drives become shame-bound. The inner self-rupture is so painful, the child must develop a "false sense." This false sense is manifested in a mask or rigid role which is either determined by the culture or by the family system's needs for balance. Over time the child identifies with the false self and becomes totally unconscious of his own true feelings, needs and wants. The shame is internalized. Shame is no longer a feeling, it is an identity. The real self has withdrawn from conscious contact.[7]

My reaction to this is to say, "Wow!" Many of us have a real self of which we are not conscious. We are not aware of it!

Earlier I suggested that we are the embodiment of a set of abilities, beliefs, assumptions, attitudes, dispositions and feelings. I don't think that there is any controversy with respect to the claim that human beings have certain types of abilities, beliefs, assumptions, dispositions and feelings. To say that they are the embodiment of these "things" is to say that human beings have bodies, and these "things" which I have listed are dependent upon

---

4. Ibid., 2.
5. Ibid.
6. Ibid., 12.
7. Ibid.

a body and a brain. A lack of oxygen to the brain results in immediate loss of consciousness. Damage to the brain caused by a stroke, Alzheimer's' disease, and similar things significant affect how a person is able to function.

What does it mean to say that we don't know ourselves? We don't know our bodies? Surely not. We don't have knowledge of our abilities, beliefs, attitudes, dispositions and feelings? Is it possible that I could be a different self with different abilities, beliefs, attitudes, dispositions and feelings? Surely not!

## CRITICISM FOUR

When Bradshaw introduced the story of Hugh, he had in mind what he has to say about masks. These masks are supposed to lead us to not be aware of whom we are. In the latter part of his book, however, he introduces a different view of what we are. He begins by mentioning a number of researchers who are studying the phenomena of "higher consciousness." He refers to a couple of psychics and the achievements they have made. He then says, "The central conclusion of all these scientists is that our full human consciousness is much more than our narrowed ego consciousness. All agree that there is a higher consciousness which transcends ego."[8] What can be said of this higher consciousness? He says, "There is also evidence that this [higher] consciousness is connected to all created consciousness."[9] Once in higher consciousness, higher power is available to us such as ESP (extra sensory perception).

Eventually he draws the following conclusion:

> What the bottom line conclusion states is that when we are in highest moments of consciousness, we are one with the universe. We are a hologram of the world. The world is a system and we are partly a whole and wholly a part. *Each of us in his own way is the universe.* This is what all the great spiritual masters have been teaching us for centuries. The ego creates separation and illusion. Once beyond ego there is no separation. We are all one. Modern science is catching up with the perennial wisdom.[10]

At one point he says, "Our true self is our God Self."[11]

8. Ibid., 228.
9. Ibid., 229.
10. Ibid.
11. Ibid., 232.

## BRADSHAW'S NEO-PLATONISM

What's going on here? Talk of the ego creating separation and illusion sounds like monism, as we have in the early Upanishads. That view is that there is only one thing that is truly real and that is Brahman. Our true Self (Atman) is Brahman. In Brahman there is no distinction between self and other, subject and object. Bradshaw says, however, that the higher consciousness which transcends ego is connected to all created consciousness. Here there is plurality. It is thus not the ultimate, not Brahman.

The best one can do here is to find an analogy. Plotinus, third century CE, is the founder of Neo-Platonism. For him the ultimate reality is the One; sometimes referred to as the Good. Here there is no distinction between subject and object and no dichotomies. The One emanates divine mind, Nous or Logos. This divine mind emanates the world which he refers to as Soul. As individuals we are emanations of the world Soul.

Bradshaw seems to think that there is a divine mind where all God selves exist in harmony. At this level ego is transcended because of this harmony. At this level our true selves, our God Selves, exist. Evidently perfect harmony means no ego and no separation. At this level "we are partly a whole and wholly a part." At this level we can also experience a higher consciousness which involves no distinction between self and object. At the highest level of reality, which Plotinus called the One, there is no distinction between self and object.

The Upanishads link Brahman to a spiritual hypothetical, a view of how to find life at its very best. It involves meditation, being aware of the true Self which is Atman/Brahman. It involves working with someone who has come to know Brahman.

Bradshaw also links his view of the true self with meditation. We are not given a precise spiritual hypothetical, a precise path to follow to find the source of life and well-being. We know, however, that it involves meditation and discovering our higher self. With meditation, Bradshaw says, "a new kind of peace and calm comes over us."[12] This peace is not tied to or dependent upon others.

> Our inner life belongs to us alone. It depends on us, not on something outside of us. We can depend on this inner world because we actually experience it. It will never go away. By having an inner life,

---

12. Ibid., 235.

> we are no longer dependent on the outside for our good feelings; we can engender them from within.[13]

There is no recognition here that our inner life and world is dependent on the brain and the proper functioning of a body. This is also a clear rejection of the Mowrer perspective that we are by nature social beings whose well-being is linked to healthy and significant relationships with others in this world as we all know it.

According to Bradshaw, shame is passed on in the family from one person to the next by necessity and no one is to blame. Speaking of his life, he says, "I'm beginning to see that everything that I have gone through had to be."[14] Everything happened of necessity. That included a father who was a drunk, the dysfunctional family of which he was apart, his own alcoholic addiction, and his suffering. The latter led to the insights and understandings that are the basis of his book. "Without my suffering, I would not be able to bear witness to an addictive society and the pain it is causing its people."[15] He then says, "From my true self point of view, my life has been perfect."[16] The best we can do is to understand what has happened.

There is no call here for people to do something so that they can improve their future. The emphasis is rather on understanding reality and how we got to the place we are. This is similar to Freud's view in that he sees the patient as a product of an unfortunate past environment. It is also like Freud in wanting to lead the patient to an insight into what caused the patient's problem. Once the insight is found the problem primarily has been solved. They also both avoid introducing questions of morality into therapy.

This is radically different from the approach of Mowrer. He had an emphasis on what ought to be done in the future to improve life. For Mowrer issues of morality are left on the table and are not avoided.

Bradshaw says, "Our true self is our God Self."[17] My true self thus does not have a body. It does not have a set of abilities, beliefs, attitudes, dispositions and feelings because my beliefs, attitudes, dispositions and feelings come in conflict with the beliefs, attitudes, dispositions and feelings of others. The conclusion is that the "true self" is not the self that I am. My true self is an embodied self with attitudes that conflict at times with the attitudes of others.

13. Ibid.
14. Ibid., 230.
15. Ibid.
16. Ibid.
17. Ibid., 232.

## SUMMARY

Element three involves beliefs and assumptions about human nature. This involves the issue of what our powers and abilities to affect things in the future, and the question of what we are as human beings. Bradshaw's religious view involves both.

When he says that from my true self point of view everything has been perfect and happened of necessity, this is the nature of the One or the Good in Plotinus. Everything emanates from the Good of necessity and nothing that is emanated influences or affects the Good. Thus from the Good's point of view he does not have power to affect and change the future.

For Bradshaw it is also true that we are spiritual beings not dependent on the physical. Lower degrees of reality cannot affect or influence higher degrees of reality. The basic criticism, of course, is that we know that our mental abilities are depend on the brain and its condition. Besides, we also know something about ourselves such as our bodies and beliefs.

# 14

# Walter Rauschenbusch

IN CHAPTER 3 THE claim was made that religious views of life can best be understood as interpretations of six elements—values, spiritual hypotheticals, human nature, rituals, authority, and a sixth element involving God, the gods, Nirvana or something similar. We then traced the various interpretations of these elements as they are found in early Hinduism, early Buddhism, biblical Judaism and early Christianity. This was followed by a critique of the interpretation of these elements as they are found in the writings of O. Hobart Mowrer, John Bradshaw, and in the teachings of Rinzai Zen. The discussion of Mowrer included a discussion of Calvin and Freud.

Mowrer focuses on personal evils which he refers to as sin. He recognizes, however, that there are also evils embedded in the society and its practices which are not personal in nature. These he refers to as corporate evils. They are evils in which a large portion of a society, or the entire society, participates. In this context participants do not consider their actions improper. For Marx capitalism was a corporate evil. Other examples: the practice of slavery, racism, and the practices by which males treat females in traditional societies.

Since in corporate evil participants consider their actions appropriate, there is neither a sense of guilt nor any necessity to hide one's actions. Corporate evil, Mowrer says, can thus be more dangerous. A sense of guilt and the fear of others becoming aware of one's guilt do not function as a cop to restrict human behavior.

We are going to focus on two religious figures who emphasized the importance of corporate evil in the twentieth century—Walter Rauschenbusch (1861–1918) and Reinhold Niebuhr (1892–1971). We will discuss Reinhold Niebuhr in the next chapter.

Rauschenbusch's *Christianity and the Social Crisis* was published in 1907. With that book he became the prime spoke-person for what has become known as the social gospel. The book was something of a barn burner. In the first three months after its publication, it was the best-selling religious book in America, except for the Bible. Fifty thousand books were sold in the first few printings. Principles of social justice came to be incorporated into the statements of faith of many denominations. It also became a part of the principles of the Federal Council of Churches, which became the National Council of Churches. This book influenced Reinhold Niebuhr and Martin Luther King Jr. The latter referred to this book as having had an "indelible imprint" on his thinking.

Walter was born in Rochester in 1861. He was the son of the professor who headed the German department at Rochester Theological Seminary, a Baptist Seminary. His father was a German immigrant who had graduated from the University of Berlin.

Sometimes to understand a thinker one needs to know something about that individual's life and the context in which the individual lived. This is true of Rauschenbusch. There are three things one should know about Rauschenbusch's life in order to understand his views: his experiences in school, his experience as a minister, and a sabbatical leave he had in Germany.

## RAUSCHENBUSCH'S SCHOOLING

Believing in the superiority of a German education, Walter's father had him attend a German Gymnasium. Walter became bilingual and to a great extent bicultural.

After graduating from the German Gymnasium, Walter did not have a university degree. He ended up taking classes at both Rochester University and Rochester Theological Seminary at the same time.

Rochester Seminary had a reputation for being conservative. His experience there, however, prepared the soil for the sprouting of a liberal theology. He became a friend of Harrison Webster, who was professor of geology and natural history at Rochester University. Webster explained to him how the new evolutionary theory, and science in general, was compatible with religious faith. He also introduced him to the writings of Henry George, a reformer who Rauschenbusch came eventually to know. George had a significant effect on him.

In his first year in seminary Rauschenbusch took a course in the gospels where he learned to interpret Scripture in its historical context. This was, in effect, an introduction to historical criticism. He saw the differences in the gospels and their linkage. The assumption that Scripture was inerrant dissolved. He knew he was embarked on a new way of understanding his faith.

His theology teacher was August Hopkins Strong, who was president of the seminary. Strong had a reputation as a conservative Calvinist, but he sought to build bridges to modern thought—something his conservative friends did not always appreciate. He sought, for example, to link modern historical criticism and evolutionary theory to traditional Calvinism.

Rauschenbusch wrote for Strong a paper on the atonement. In it he was critical of the traditional ways of understanding it, which included Strong's own interpretation. He criticized it on moral grounds—something that fits with his later liberalism. Strong regarded suffering and punishment for sin as something that is demanded by God's holiness, which constituted the reason for the cross. For Rauschenbusch this was incompatible with God's nature. Strong was bothered by Rauschenbusch's paper, but he respected him as a scholar. Eventually he ended up hiring him to fill the position his father had.

This pattern Rauschenbusch followed was much like a pattern this author followed. He went to conservative Baptist seminary, Northern Baptist Seminary. He was assigned Strong's Systematic Theology for a class in theology. He took a class on the Synoptic Gospels in Greek where he came to appreciate historical criticism. He wrote a paper on the atonement attacking the traditional view on moral grounds. The paper took issue with the point of view of the professor who taught the class.

## HIS JOB AS PASTOR

After graduating from seminary Rauschenbusch accepted a job as pastor of the Second German Baptist Church in New York City. It was an old church of working class immigrants with 125 parishioners. It sat adjacent to Hell's Kitchen—an area of New York City that earned its name.

Rauschenbusch came to know in an intimate way the poverty and suffering of its people. A huge number of immigrants were coming into the city on a regular basis. Between 1880 and 1890 there were nearly six million immigrants.[1] That's about fifty thousand a month. In Hell's Kitchen they lived mostly in overly crowded, poorly vented tenement houses. These houses were incubators for diseases often fatal—typhoid fever, cholera, and tuberculosis.

He had to face men who were pleading for jobs—sometimes unable to get hospital care for their families. He had to perform funerals for children whose deaths were attributed to the poverty in which they lived. Government had not developed tools to protect workers in their places of work, to protect people in their tenement houses, nor to protect the food they bought in the marketplace.

It became obvious to Rauschenbusch that there was a gross injustice that produced Hell's Kitchen. After a year at Second Baptist he wrote to relatives in Germany that his father's faith was not adequate to address the problems of our modern world.

Rauschenbusch became aware that Hell's Kitchen was not a unique place. It was replicated in many urban areas because of industrialization of the economy. Complimenting this experience as pastor, he was influenced by material he read and by friends who he came to know. He read Sidney and Beatrice Webb who were British socialists; Edward Bellamy's utopian novel *Looking Backward* (1888). This novel depicted a future ideal world without the sins of wealth and poverty. It included Joseph Riis's study *How the Other Half Lived* (1890). This exposed the misery of tenement living in New York City. He also read Karl Marx and Frederick Engels, despite their hostility to Christianity.

Rauschenbusch also came to know some of the Christian reformers of the late nineteenth century—Henry George, William Gladden, Josiah Strong, Richard Ely and W. D. P. Bliss. Henry George was a reformer who ran for mayor of New York City when Rauschenbusch moved to New York. William Gladden was a minister. His theology was probably the first one to embrace the importance of what was referred to as social Christianity. In 1876 he published *Working People and Their Employers*, a very influential work. He considered it a role of the church to address the economic problems of the time. Both he and George were concerned about the inequality in the distribution of wealth.

---

1. 123 See SUSPS, "Population Numbers."

Richard Ely was an Episcopalian who was an economist with a PhD from the University of Heidelberg. He found in the teachings of Jesus an ideal of justice that he believed should shape the character of society.

W. D. P. Bliss was a reformer who was influenced by British socialism. In 1889 he started the Society for Christian Socialists. Socialism, he said, was where the fatherhood of God and the brotherhood of man are recognized. It is where the teachings of Jesus—love your neighbor as yourself and the golden rule—are recognized. He did not embrace a top-down view of socialism, as found in England, but what might be called a bottom-up approach.

Bliss had an influence on many. Under his influence Rauschenbusch started to refer to himself as a socialist.

## SABBATICAL LEAVE IN GERMANY

When he was in seminary Rauschenbusch recognized that he had a hearing problem. He discovered that this was something that he inherited. By 1891 it was getting worse and starting to affect his ministry. He decided to leave the ministry and spend some time in Germany. When he returned, he thought that he might focus on writing. He had written articles for Baptist publications. For a year and a half he had edited a Christian newspaper with a friend, Leighton Williams. The paper gave him a chance to address issues of social reform.

He announced his resignation to his church in January 1891. To his amazement his congregation refused his resignation. It offered to help pay his expenses in Germany and to pay for an interim pastor.

Nine months in Germany gave him time to renew acquaintances, to read, and to reflect on his theology. Prior to his trip to Germany he had started to use the phrase "kingdom of God" to refer to what a just society was like. He had heard someone use the phrase in the Lord's Prayer, "Thy kingdom come, Thy will be done," and use it in such a way as to apply it to the world in which we live. That stuck in Rauschenbusch's mind. The history here is not clear. Apparently, however, it was in the context of his sabbatical leave in Germany that he came to see the kingdom of God as the focus of the teachings of Jesus. It was the concern not only of Jesus, but a central concern of his followers. It also tied together all of the religious concerns that Rauschenbusch had. This included, he said, the saving of the lost, the teaching of the young, the pastoral care of the poor and frail, the quickening of starved intellects, the study of the Bible, church union, political reform, the reorganization of the industrial system, international peace—it was all covered by the reign of God on earth.[2]

Germany was the home of the two great liberal theologians, Albert Ritschl and Adolph von Harnack. Ritschl died a couple years earlier, but his student Harnack was very active. Since Ritschl also emphasized the kingdom of God, the question naturally arises as to whether Rauschenbusch derived this emphasis from Ritschl. He is sometimes referred to as a follower of Ritschl.

It is easy to see that they have something in common. Consider the following statement from Ritschl: "The religious motive of ethical action lies here, that the Kingdom of God which is our task to realize, represents also the highest good which God destines for us as our supramundane goal."[3] The phrase "supramundane goal" is not one that Rauschenbusch would use, but the statement sounds much like Rauschenbusch. There is a difference, however. It lies in Rauschenbusch's understanding of the nature of what is included in the Christian's task of achieving the highest good. For Rauschenbusch it included the study of society and its political and economic system. A study from the perspective of the ideals of justice and equality, as Ely emphasized. This is not what Ritschl had in mind.

Rauschenbusch's criticism of Ritschl was kind. He said, "Ritschl has done more than anyone else to put the idea [of the kingdom of God] in the front of German theology, but he does not get beyond a few general ideas. He was born too early to get sociological ideas."[4] In other words, he did not embrace the social gospel.

Harnack was the student of Ritschl who became a lead spokesperson for liberal theology in Germany. He also had an emphasis on the kingdom of God. He said that it has a triple meaning. It is something supernatural, i.e., a gift from above; a purely religious blessing, and an important religious experience. Of this experience he says, "It permeates and dominates his whole existence, because sin is forgiven and misery banished."[5] This triple

2. 124 Minus, *Walter Rauschenbusch*, 81.
3. Ritschl, *Christian Doctrine*, 205–6.
4. Rauschenbusch, *Theology for the Social Gospel*, 138.
5. Harnack, *What Is Christianity?*, 61–62.

meaning links the kingdom of God to personal redemption, but not to social redemption and the social gospel.

The political conservatism of the liberals in Germany bothered Rauschenbusch. This involved an attachment to German nationalism, and sometimes anti-Semitism.

## HIS LIBERAL THEOLOGY: VALUES

Rauschenbusch seeks to derive his understanding of values from the life and ministry of Jesus. This requires, he says, understanding the context in which he lived and the roots of his thoughts. In *Christianity and the Social Crisis* Rauschenbusch traces these roots back to the Hebrew prophets.

Contemporary Christians, he said, do not understand the prophets very well. Contemporary Christians focus on the religion of the individual, whereas the prophets focused on the nation. Churches consider sin in terms of a lack of piety—intemperance, being unchaste, and misuse of the tongue. The contrast between this and the prophets is clear. "The twin-evil against which the prophets launched the condemnation of Jehovah was injustice and oppression."[6] At one point Rauschenbusch says that the prophets demanded one thing and only one thing—righteousness.[7]

To say that God demanded only righteousness is, in effect, to say that God demanded only what it moral. What Rauschenbusch endorsed was referred to earlier as a liberal view of the divine command theory. One ought to do what God commands because God embodies the highest moral principles. It was this assumption that was behind his seminary paper which was critical of traditional views of the atonement.

## JESUS AND HIS TEACHINGS

For Rauschenbusch the message of the prophets came to be embodied in Jesus and his teachings. To understand him, Rauschenbusch said, one must see him as having a revolutionary consciousness. Through him God was to "put down the mighty and exalt them of low degree" (Luke 1:52). "The first would be last and the last would be first" (Mark 10:31). This was said in the context of a religious state, a type of theocracy. It was thus revolutionary.

---

6. Rauschenbusch, *Christianity and the Social Crisis in the 21st Century*, 6.
7. Ibid., 4.

All of the teachings of Jesus, Rauschenbusch said, were linked to the concept of the kingdom of God. From the point of view of the elements of religion, it would appear that all of the important values were embedded in that concept.

It needs to be kept in mind that these values are not spiritualized. Rauschenbusch considered that kingdom to be a transformation of society on earth. He considered Paul's view as "an immediate spiritualization of the entire cosmos."[8] Paul's outlook, Rauschenbusch says, is void of social elements and the material ceases to exist. Rauschenbusch believed that in the Apocalypse the new would be a glorified old earth. The Lord's Prayer says, "They will be done on earth." Nature would continue and be free of the stunting power of sin.[9]

In discussing Jesus, Rauschenbusch says that the primary values of God's kingdom were love, service, and equality.[10]

The love commandment has equality built into it. One is to love one's neighbor as oneself. The neighbor is just as important as oneself.

In justifying his emphasis on service Rauschenbusch refers to Matthew 20:25–28. Here the message is that among the Gentiles, the rulers lord it over their people. In his kingdom, however, they are to be servants of one another.

Related to the emphasis on the three basic principles is the fact that God's kingdom, Rauschenbusch says, does not have hard and fast laws. This fits the view of law found in Mark. There we find law is regarded as a means of maximizing human well-being.

Rauschenbusch mentions in his book *Christianity and the Social Crisis* that there are different understandings of the kingdom of God among scholars. This was probably an illusion to the views of Albert Schweitzer. He says, however, that he does not have the time to address that issue in this book. This issue arises again, however, in his *Theology for the Social Gospel* (1918). There he does not refer to Schweitzer by name. Instead, he refers to a group of very able scholars as having made Jesus into an apocalyptic enthusiast.[11] Rauschenbusch's response is to say that Q is the earliest source. He then goes on to say that it contains the least amount of apocalyptic material.[12] He

---

8. Rauschenbusch, *Christianity and the Social Crisis in the 21st Century*, 89.
9. Rauschenbusch, *Theology for the Social Gospel*, 90.
10. Rauschenbusch, *Christianity and the Social Crisis in the 21st Century*, 56–57.
11. Rauschenbusch, *Theology for the Social Gospel*, 218.
12. Ibid., 219.

also quotes Harnack who said that a study of Q will undermine the position of those who see Jesus as an apocalyptic prophet.[13]

This issue was discussed in chapter 9. The point made there was that there is evidence on both sides of this issue which cannot be easily settled.

## SPIRITUAL HYPOTHETICALS

The word "gospel" means good news. For Rauschenbusch there was a personal gospel and a social gospel. Most of his emphasis, however, was on the social gospel.

The proclamation of good news implies a spiritual hypothetical, a view wherein lies human well-being. Spiritual hypotheticals, however, also take a negative form, a view of what leads to human degradation and suffering. For Rauschenbusch, Hell's Kitchen was a symbol of the human degradation and suffering brought by the industrial revolution. The question for him, then, was what caused Hell's Kitchen?

His answer is given in chapter 5 of *Christianity and the Social Crisis*. Before the industrial revolution, he says, there were towns where craftsmen worked in their home and honed their skill with simple tools. They hired apprentices and journeymen to help him. The craftsmen joined together to form guilds to help one another and promote their self-interests. The towns functioned as barrier reefs to protect their craftsmen and their shop owners from predators and external competition.

The machine then arrived. It could make what a hundred or a thousand craftsmen could make. Their rich owners functioned as a storm surge to wash out the barrier reefs protecting the towns. Capitalism and competition started to rule the day. The machine promised wealth and to banish want and the fear of want. The poor, however, suffered at the hand of the rich. Pay was based on an inverse proportion to need. Those in most need worked for the least amount of money. Those who needed it the least would end up with more. Large cities developed and areas like Hell's Kitchen came into being. The rich used their power to control government and the economy. The United States without an established social system was particularly vulnerable to the rise of capitalism. Rauschenbusch quotes Gustav Schmoller, who said, "All experts agree that no country has such a plutocracy as the United States."[14]

13. Ibid.
14. Rauschenbusch, *Christianity and the Social Crisis in the 21st Century*, 183.

The spiritual hypothetical is that greed, capitalism and the machine can produce suffering and misery. Neither the machine nor did capitalism produced the greed, but they enabled it to flourish.

One answer to this problem was state socialism as found in England. Rauschenbusch, Bliss and a number of other reformers in America endorsed socialism, but rejected that top-down type of socialism. They wanted to build socialism from the ground up. The ideal is for people to come together in brotherly love, working together and sharing profits with fellow workers. Love and equality ought to be the ideals that govern the economic system.

Equality does not mean everyone has the same amount of money or success. He refers to the family as an institution where there can be equality in status, each person is equally important. Differences in sex, knowledge and abilities can coexist with equality of status. The same kind of thing should exist in society. Real democracy, however, requires a large sharing of the wealth of the society. "Approximate equality is the only enduring function of political democracy."[15] Much concentration of wealth in the hands of few means too much power in the hands of few. This undermines equality and democracy. This is similar to the views of Reinhold Niebuhr, who we will be discussing next.

Earlier we saw that for Rauschenbusch the kingdom of God was the focus of the teachings of Jesus. In emphasizing the social gospel, however, Rauschenbusch did not intend to undermine the importance of the personal gospel. There are differences, however. In talking about sin with respect to the social gospel, he says,

> Attention is concentrated on questions of public morality, on wrongs done by whole classes or professions of men, on sin which enervate and submerge entire mill towns or agricultural states. These sins have been side-stepped by the old theology. We now have to make up for a fatal failure in past teaching.[16]

The proper way to read this is to say that social gospel focuses on corporate evil instead of personal sin.

In his *Theology for the Social Gospel* he says that it is not sufficient to put the two gospels side by side. Rather, he says, there must be a synthesis of the two.[17] In the tradition of pietism, Rauschenbusch considers personal

---

15. Ibid., 203.
16. Rauschenbusch, *Theology for the Social Gospel*, 36.
17. Ibid., 144.

redemption to involve a religious experience and a change in one's character. He then goes on to say that any religious experience that does not have a social dimension is not a Christian experience.[18] "When we submit to God," he says, "we submit to the common good. Salvation is the socializing of the soul."[19]

Note that there is an analogy here between what Rauschenbusch says about personal redemption and what Mowrer says. Both emphasize the importance of the social dimension of life. A person, Mowrer says, "is preeminently a social creature and that he lives or dies, psychologically personally as a function of the openness, community, relatedness, and integrity which by good actions he attains and by evil actions destroys."[20]

In speaking of personal salvation Rauschenbusch talks about the problem of guilt, the burden of sin, and the need of forgiveness. Voluntary obedience to God, he says, brings freedom.[21] Here we have a spiritual hypothetical.

With respect to the personal gospel faith involves voluntary obedience to God. With respect to the social gospel, he says,

> It is faith to assert the feasibility of a fairly righteous and fraternal social order. In the midst of a despotic and predatory industrial life, it is faith to stake our business future on the proposition that fairness, kindness, and fraternity will work. When war inflames a nation, it is faith to believe that a peaceable disposition is a workable international policy.[22]

Note Rauschenbusch is taking the personal ideals of fraternity and kindness and applying them to the industrial world, to the business world, and to international affairs. In the next chapter we will find that Reinhold Niebuhr is critical of this point of view. Niebuhr would find the perspective of this paragraph naïve. This author agrees.

---

18. Ibid., 97.
19. Ibid., 99.
20. Mowrer, *Crisis*, 44.
21. Rauschenbusch, *Theology for the Social Gospel*, 95.
22. Ibid., 102.

## A CRITIQUE

There are three issues that deserve to be discussed. One, does Rauschenbusch have an overly optimistic view of human nature? Two, how good is his scholarship with respect to Scripture and history? Three, is he right that love and competition are incompatible?

It is a common criticism of nineteenth-century liberalism that it is has an overly optimistic view of human nature. This belongs to element three in the elements of religion. In the late nineteenth century there was a therapeutic type of Christianity that was made popular by Russell Conwell.[23] It considered Christian faith as a key to a successful, prosperous life. Rauschenbusch took issue with that. He was affected by Tolstoy's *My Religion* and came to see voluntary self-sacrifice as important to the Christian life. Suffering, he believed, could be redemptive. The cross of Jesus he thought was an example of this.

On the other hand, he does take seriously the parables in the Synoptic Gospels that likened the kingdom to grain which grows and matures until it reaches its fulfillment and is reaped. That makes growth built into the historical process. It forces a person to be ultimately optimistic about the future. That optimism occasionally manifests itself.

In his book *A Theology for the Social Gospel*, Rauschenbusch emphasizes the reality and importance of sin. At one point he recognizes what he calls the kingdom of evil. In this context he likens society, and groups within a society, to organisms in which individual parts need to be understood in terms of the whole organism. This is similar to Niebuhr. In this context he says, "The apparent free and unrelated acts of individuals are also the acts of the social group."[24] That is to say, the individual is to be understood in terms of the larger group of which he is a part. He then goes on to say, "When the social group is evil, evil is all over."[25] That does not sound like an optimistic view of human nature.

Finally, his description of the role of faith with respect to the social gospel shows an overly optimistic approach to dealing with corporate evil. We will discuss this problem in the next chapter on Reinhold Niebuhr.

The second issue involves the question of how good is his scholarship with respect to Scripture and history. In his discussion in *Christianity and*

---

23. Evans, *Kingdom*, 78.
24. Rauschenbusch, *Theology for the Social Gospel*, 81.
25. Ibid.

*the Social Crisis in the 21st Century*, Stanley Hauerwas says, "[This] book is, I think, a sermon seeking to convict Christians of our sins as well as call us to the redeeming work of the kingdom of God."[26] This seems right. The standards for judging a sermon differ, however, from the standards for judging a scholarly work.

It is a mistake to see this book as a scholarly work on Scripture or on history. Those issues are empirical in nature. They require weighing evidence on both sides of the issues. This Rauschenbusch does not do. In general he avoids discussing controversial issues and discussing the sides on these issues.

A sermon needs to communicate effectively with its audience. The success of the book in the marketplace indicates that it did that. A sermon also should speak with passion and eloquence on something important. With respect to social justice the book does this. Rauschenbusch speaks with passion and eloquence and influenced the Christian community. A number of denominations were led to adopt a social justice emphasis into their statements of faith.

The third relevant issue is whether he is right that love and competition are incompatible. Is capitalism compatible with the commandment to love one's neighbor as oneself?

Consider games. Games involve competition to win. Do they rule out love between competitors? That raises the question as to what love is. Rauschenbusch does not give us a definition. Can one talk about love in the context of a capitalistic economy? The common view is that the command to love is *agape*. That would mean that the command to love one's neighbor is a command to act for the well-being of others. The command to love can properly be considered as a command to respect others and to act for their well-being.

Respect for an individual and a commitment to the well-being of that individual are compatible with competing with that individual in the context of a game. The same is true in legislative bodies. Legislators compete over which bills should be passed and which laws ought to come into effect. This is like competition in the marketplace. Respect and a commitment to the well-being of a competitor are compatible.

Capitalism, he says, produces two classes. This emphasis on class, however, can be misleading. It may imply that owners cannot really take seriously the well-being of their employees and the affects that their goods

---

26. Ibid., 173.

or services have on society. It may imply that owners will function as members of a class as opposed to normal human beings who are concerned with how their actions affect others.

Owners are human beings that can be concerned about something other than just money. They can be concerned about the well-being of their employees and the contribution their products or their services make, or do not make, to the larger community.

Besides, when a company is concerned with its long-term well-being, it should see that its own long-term well-being is linked to having employees who like their job and the company. It is also linked to having customers who like the company and their products. Thus the interests of owners, employees and the customers do not necessarily differ.

Society benefits when a company can provide service at a good price which benefits the society. Besides, the desire to compete can result in innovations that are beneficial to society. Producing better products at a better price is good for everyone, except the competitor who is unable to compete. The challenge to the loser is to innovate and develop skills in order to compete in the marketplace. The challenge of the society is to have a safety net for those who lose in the competition.

## SUMMARY

In our contemporary world it is assumed that a Christian liberal will be concerned about the issues of poverty and social justice. It was not always so. Rauschenbusch along with cohorts such as Henry George, William Gladden, Richard Ely, Josiah Strong, and W. D. P. Bliss initiated a movement which changed the trajectory of Christian liberalism in America. Germany did not participate. England was ahead of America.

The society of that day was very much a Protestant society. All of these reformers were Protestants. Protestantism was often linked in their minds to an Anglo-Saxon tradition which they often considered superior. At one point Rauschenbusch heard a Roman Catholic priest that impressed him. Catholicism, however, did not have much of an impact on these reformers or upon the society of its day. Rauschenbusch never mentions a rabbi. This was a generation before Jewish immigrants started to have an impact on American culture. The concept of religious pluralism never seemed to enter their minds.

## Part 4—Theological Issues

The development of Rauschenbusch as a liberal is interesting. It raises the question of when a person is a liberal. In seminary he learned the difference between science and religion, and learned to integrate them. He learned to appreciate the historical critical approach to interpreting Scripture. As a student under Augustus Hopkins Strong, he wrote a paper that attacked the traditional view of the atonement on moral grounds.

Those changes would normally result in a person being classified as a liberal. He was not perceived as a liberal, however. His early sermons at Second Baptist Church focused on personal salvation, as a conservative would. He attended the meetings of Dwight Moody and enjoyed them. What resulted in a switch in perceptions? He came to see Jesus and his disciples to be focused on the kingdom of God. A commitment to this kingdom meant a war against corporate evil in all its shapes and form. This didn't mean giving up on the importance of personal salvation. It meant a call to awaken the church to a mission that the church had overlooked.

# 15

# Reinhold Niebuhr

WHEN WE CONSIDER SPIRITUAL hypotheticals applicable to society as a whole and the institutions within them, then thought ought to be given as to the kind of thing a society is and the nature of the institutions within it. This is the concern of Reinhold Niebuhr's book *Moral Man and Immoral Society* (1932).

Niebuhr was a minister and theologian born in Wright City, Missouri, the son of German immigrants and a German Evangelical pastor. He earned a bachelor of divinity degree and a master of arts degree from the Yale Divinity School. In 1915 he was ordained a pastor. The German Evangelical mission board then sent him to serve at Bethel Evangelical Church in Detroit, Michigan. In 1928, Niebuhr left Detroit to become professor of practical theology at Union Theological Seminary in New York, where he spent the rest of his career.

He came out of seminary a theological liberal and pacifist, but eventually came to reject both and came to be identified as a Christian realist. Rauschenbusch was also the son of a German immigrant. His experience as a pastor next to Hell's Kitchen pushed him in a liberal direction. Niebuhr's experience in Detroit, as a liberal, pushed him to be more moderate.

Even though Niebuhr was a minister and his primary focus was on religious ethics, he became popular in the secular arena. He was influential both in the United States and abroad; he helped found the liberal Americans for Democratic Action (ADA) in 1947. His ideas influenced George Kennan, Hans Morgenthau, and Arthur Schlesinger Jr. As a realist he argued for the importance of power to contain the communist expansion. Such concerns helped bring about the Cold War.

His *Moral Man and Immoral Society* was published in 1932. In 1960 he was approached about republishing this book. He said that he has changed many of his views since then, but that the underlining argument he believed was sound and relevant. He thus approved its republication.

In the preface written in 1960, he says, "The central thesis was, and is, that the Liberal Movement both religious and secular seemed to be unconscious of the basic difference between the morality of individuals and the morality of collectives, whether races, classes or nations."[1]

## THE MORAL PROBLEM OF COLLECTIVES

He uses the word "collective" to refer to all kinds of groups without defining exactly what the parameters are for being a collective. I don't think that all tall, brown hair males would be a collective. Why? Of collectives, he says, self-interest is inevitable. It appears for him that a group has to have self-interest to be a collective. Consider all persons between five and six feet tall. I don't think that he would consider them as a collective or as a social group because they lack self-interest. That seems to be a necessity for him to consider something to be a collective or a social group.

We have seen that Mowrer draws a distinction personal evils or sins, and corporate evils. Actions of social groups that have self-interest would not qualify as personal sins. They would qualify, however, as a type of corporate evil. One way of describing Niebuhr's concerns is say that he wants to understand corporate actions and how they are to be understood as good and evil.

Collectives differ from individuals, he says. Individuals are capable of viewing a social situation where their self-interest is at stake with objectivity; they can then prefer the well-being of others to their own. The contrast he draws is this: "But all these achievements are more difficult, if not impossible, for human societies and social groups."[2] If social groups by nature have self-interests, a group could not give up all of its self-interests. It would cease to exist. It does not follow from this, however, that on a given occasion it might act contrary to its self-interests. On a given occasion for

---

1. Niebuhr, *Moral Man*, xxiii.
2. Ibid., xxv.

moral reasons a group may act contrary to its self-interests. Paying taxes may be such an occasion.

Since a society is made of many groups with self-interests that often conflict with one another, social harmony without conflict, he says, is impossible. In fact, he goes further than this and says that a society is always in a state of war.[3] Democracy, he says, does not solve this problem because the economic interests of commercial classes prevent government from placing restraints on economic activity.[4] This sounds like Rauschenbusch. The US legislature, however, has the constitutional authority to regulate interstate commerce according to Article 1, Section 8, of the Constitution. It has passed laws that do this on a number of occasions. To say that such regulations cannot affect economic activity is too strong of a statement.

What does justice mean when a society is composed of self-interested groups with conflicting self-interests? Justice, he says, "is established by the assertion of power against power."[5] It is the disproportionate power in society that is the real root of social injustice. In other words, the key to justice in society is it to have a balance of power among self-interested groups.

How then is the problem of injustice to be addressed? If disproportionate power in society is the root of injustice, the use of power is obviously necessary to obtain justice. His criticism of religious and secular liberals is that they fail to recognize the necessity of power. The only way to restrain power is to use power. Rational discussions and compromises can play a role and function, but by themselves will not affect the structure of a society. They have value, but by themselves they are not sufficient to significantly change a society.

## A POSITIVE CRITIQUE

There are some good things and some criticisms that can be said about Niebuhr's point of view. Let's consider the good first.

One way to assess the truth of what he has to say is to consider the major advances in society with respect to justice that took place in the twentieth century. There were at least three major advances in America: (1) Women's suffrage; the recognition that women are equal before the law. (2) The recognition by government of the right of workers to form labor

3. Ibid., 19.
4. Ibid., 14.
5. Ibid., 31.

unions and to bargain and strike. (3) The improvement in the power and status of blacks in the '50s and '60s.

In each case there was an injustice rooted in power—the power of males over females; the power of industry over its workers; and the power of whites over blacks. In each case rhetoric and reason played a role to check power, but the use of power was crucial.

In 1848, a group of abolitionist activists gathered in Seneca Falls, New York, to discuss the problem of women's rights. Out of that gathering came a statement of women's rights. It said, "We hold these truths to be self-evident that all men and women are created equal, that they are endowed by their creator with certain inalienable rights; that among these are life, liberty, and the pursuit of happiness."[6] What this meant, among other things, was that women should have the right to vote.

On August 26, 1920, the Nineteenth Amendment to the Constitution was finally ratified, enfranchising all American women. For the first time, they, like men, deserved the rights and responsibilities of citizenship. It took the power of government and a constitutional amendment to bring this about.

In the nineteenth century, Hell's Kitchen was a symbol of the power that industry had over workers. Reformers, such as Rauschenbusch, recognized the problem but were not successful in doing much about it. The union movement, which started in the mid-nineteenth century, represented the attempt of workers to push back and restrain the power of industry. Workers found meager success. The first significant success came in 1935 when the National Labor Relations Act, NLRA, or Wagner Act, became US federal law. It protected the right of employees to discuss organizing in the work place; to engage in collective bargaining, and to strike in support of their demands. As Niebuhr said, to restrain power one needs to use power.

After the Civil War, Jim Crow laws developed in the South. These were laws to keep blacks and whites separate in public schools, public places, and public transportation. Restrooms, restaurants, and drinking fountains were all segregated. The US military was also segregated. The difference between the North and the South was that the North was segregated on the basis of conventional practices, whereas the South had laws as well as practices to enforce the segregation.

---

6. See "Fight for Women's Suffrage," http://www.history.com/topics/womens-history/the-fight-for-womens-suffrage.

Those who defended the laws enforcing segregation argued that separate but equal access to public facilities was constitutional. To support their case they referred to the Plessy v. Ferguson (1896) case in which the Supreme Court placed its stamp of approval on separate but equal access to public facilities. In 1954 the Supreme Court struck down the separate but equal principle with respect to public education in the Brown v. Board of Education case.

Later, in 1964, came the Civil Rights Act which outlawed discrimination against racial, ethnic, national and religious minorities, and women. To this was added the Voting Rights Act of 1965 that outlawed discriminatory voting practices that had been responsible for disenfranchising African Americans.

In all three cases disproportionate power led to injustice. In all three cases the government stepped in on the side of the less powerful to improve the balance of power. Perfect balance has never been achieved. But Niebuhr's point that an imbalance of power leads to injustice and a balance of power leads to greater justice seems to be the case.

In the middle of the twentieth century the gospel of communism and its support by the Soviet Union was a threat to American sovereignty and well-being. In that context Niebuhr argued that power had to be used to restrain power. From that perspective the cold war policy developed. Fortunately, it was successful.

## A NEGATIVE CRITIQUE

Obviously a society has groups of individuals with conflicting interests. Conflict seems to be built into the nature of societies. An important question is whether groups with different interests can focus their interests so that their interests harmonize as opposed to conflict. Consider three cases.

Companies often figure their value is based on the sum total value of their stock. When the total value of the stock of a company goes up, it is considered as having more value. When it goes down, it is considered as having less value.

Consider a professional sports team. Should the value of a sports team be determined on the basis of its win-loss record in a given season? A smart investor would look to the future and try to determine how the team is likely to function in the future. It would evaluate the talent in the team and evaluate the nature of the organization.

The same applies to a company. As I have argued before, a company wants good employees who like their job and consumers who like their products or their services. It thus pays for management to respect their employees and treat them well, and to make good products that consumers like. Management, of course, must also be concerned about the interests of stock owners who are going to expect a profit from their investments. There is nothing about a company, however, to rule out the possibility of satisfying the interests of stockowners, employees, and consumers; to harmonize the interests of the three groups. What is important is to understand the company from a long range point of view and not just the value of stock at a particular time.

Consider a second case. For a significant period of time American made automobiles were inferior to those made in Japan and Europe. Over a period of time the management of GM and similar companies developed a fraternal relationship with employees and their unions. This was the kind of thing that Rauschenbusch would have considered to be important. The problem was that the consumer was not a part of that fraternity. They were being cheated by getting inferior products. This became clear when Japanese companies got into the automobile business and exported their automobiles into the United States. The point of the case is to recognize that a company ought to take into consideration the well-being of both its employees and its consumers.

Consider a third case. Niebuhr recognizes that each country has self-interest and these interests often conflict. The challenge is to find situations where interests do not conflict but harmonize.

There is an important case where the interests of a number of countries did not conflict. Consider the Marshall plan, the name given to the Economic Cooperation Act which was proposed in 1947, after World War II, and passed by Congress in 1948. The program was devised and run by General George Marshall, secretary of state. Its purpose was to help the countries of Europe recover from the devastating effects of the war—to address the problems of hunger and poverty, to prevent chaos from overwhelming the countries; to build up the infrastructure and the economies. He believed political stability required revitalized economies.

The United States, Marshall said, would provide funds. He invited other countries to participate in this rebuilding effort. The Soviet Union refused. It was up to the European countries to determine how the money would be divided up and exactly how it would be used. Sixteen nations were provided 13.3 billion dollars. This was in addition to 13 billion in emergency aid that was provided immediately after the war in 1945.[7]

The Marshall Plan ended in 1952. At that time the economies of Western Europe were in better shape than they were before the war began.

Here we have a peculiar blend of self-interest and humanitarian interest. Building up and helping a competitor is not the kind of self-interest Niebuhr had in mind. There is no way to weigh the balance of these two interests. The United States had self interest in having economies with which it can trade and exchange goods. The United States also knew that communists could take advantage of a chaotic situation. They could plant seeds and grow cells that furthered their cause. At the same time, observing what the war had done to buildings, bridges, and to the people who felt both hopelessness and hunger aroused interest in providing humanitarian aid. The danger in Niebuhr's ethical point of view is that it can lead to overlooking the ways that groups and nations can have interests that harmonize and be mutually beneficial.

## SUMMARY

Mowrer's distinction between personal sin and corporate evil is an important one. It's analogous to Rauschenbusch's distinction between a personal gospel and a social gospel; it's also analogous to Niebuhr's distinction between personal ethics and social ethics. The effects of the industrial revolution led many individuals to be aware and concerned about corporate evil. From this developed reformers such as Marx, Engels, Booth, and the socialists in England. Rauschenbusch belonged to a set of Protestant reformers, who spoke of social salvation, social gospel, and social justice. All of them identified with ideals of love and justice which they identified with Jesus. All were concerned with transforming society to better reflect the ideals of love and justice. In general they rejected the model of socialism found in England, but they differed with respect to whether the free enterprise system is consistent with the ideals of love and justice.

Niebuhr's claim is that love is a personal value. It is important to distinguish the morality of collectives such as nations, classes and social groups from the morality of individuals. Morality for collectives is justice, and justice involves a balance of power among self-interested groups.

7. See the Marshall Plan, George C. Marshall Foundation, http://www.marshallfoundation.org/TheMarshallPlan.htm.

## Part 4 — Theological Issues

Injustice involves an imbalance of power, and it requires power to address this imbalance.

We saw that Niebuhr's perspective sheds light on advances in social justice in the twentieth century. Advances in the status of women, workers, and blacks were a product of the government using power to restrain power. This same policy played a role to restrain the power of the Soviet Union in what was called the Cold War.

The criticism of Niebuhr is that he tended to overlook the ways that the self-interests of collectives can be directed so that they harmonize with one another, instead of conflict.

# Bibliography

Abraham, William J. *The Divine Inspiration of Scripture*. Oxford: Oxford University Press, 1981.
Anderson, Bernard W. *Understanding the Old Testament*. Englewood Cliffs, NJ: Prentice Hall, 1957.
Aquinas, Thomas. "Summa Theologica, Part I." In *Basic Writings of Saint Thomas Aquinas*, vol. 1, edited by Anton C. Pegis. New York: Random House, 1944.
Aslan, Reza. *Zealot: The Life and Times of Jesus of Nazareth*. New York: Random House, 2013.
Barth, Karl. *Church Dogmatics*. Vols. 1 & 4. Edinburgh: T. & T. Clark, 1956, 1958.
———. *Dogmatics in Outline*. New York: Harper, 1959.
———. *Evangelical Theology: An Introduction*. New York: Holt, Reinhart & Winston, 1963.
Blackstone, William T. *The Problem of Religious Knowledge*. Englewood Cliffs, NJ: Prentice Hall, 1963.
Bonhoeffer, Dietrich. *Life Together*. New York: Harper, 1954.
Borg, Marcus. *Evolution of the Word*. New York: HarperCollins, 2012.
———. *Jesus: A New Vision*. San Francisco: Harper & Row, 1987.
Bradshaw, John. *Bradshaw On: The Family; A Revolutionary Way of Self-Discovery*. Deerfield Beach, FL: Health Communications, 1988.
Brown, D. Mackenzie. *Ultimate Concern: Tillich in Dialogue*. New York: Harper & Row, 1965.
Burtt, E. A., ed. *Teachings of the Compassionate Buddha*. New York: New American Library, 1955.
Conze, Edward. *Buddhism: Its Essence and Development*. New York: Harper & Row, 1975.
Corliss, Richard. "Schleiermacher's Hermeneutic and Its Critics." *Religious Studies* 29 (1993) 363–79.
Cross, Frank Moore. *Canaanite Myth and Hebrew Epic*. 2nd ed. Cambridge: Harvard University Press, 1981.
CRTA (Center for Reformed Theology and Apologetics). "Definition of the Council of Chalcedon (451 AD)." http://www.reformed.org/documents/chalcedon.html.
Davis, Steven T. *The Debate about the Bible: Inerrancy versus Infallibility*. Philadelphia: Westminster, 1977.

# Bibliography

Dienhart, John William. *A Cognitive Approach to the Ethics of Counseling Psychology.* Washington, DC: University Press of America, 1982.

Driver, S. R. *An Introduction to the Literature of the Old Testament.* Rev ed. New York: Scribner, 1948.

Ehrman, Bart. *Jesus: Apocalyptic Prophet of the New Millennium.* New York: Oxford University Press, 1999.

———. *Misquoting Jesus: The Story behind Who Changed the Bible and Why.* New York: HarperCollins, 2005.

Evans, Christopher H. *The Kingdom Is Always Coming: A Life of Walter Rauschenbusch.* Waco, TX: Baylor University Press, 2010.

Feenstra, Ronald. "Reconsidering Kenotic Christology." In *Trinity, Incarnation, and Atonement*, edited by Ronald Feenstra and Cornelius Plantinga Jr., 128–52. Notre Dame: University of Notre Dame Press, 1989.

Flew, Anthony, ed. *Logic and Language.* 1st and 2nd series. Oxford: Blackwell, 1951 and 1959.

Flew, Anthony, and Alasdair MacIntyre, eds. *New Essays in Philosophical Theology.* London: SCM, 1955.

Friedman, Richard Elliott. *Who Wrote the Bible?* New York: HarperCollins, 1989.

Geisler, Norman, ed. *Inerrancy.* Grand Rapids: Zondervan, 1980.

Glasser, William. *Reality Therapy.* New York: Harper & Row, 1965.

Gotobed, Julian. "Walter Rauschenbusch (1861–1918)." With material submitted by Michelle Charles. http://people.bu.edu/wwildman/bce/rauschenbusch.htm.

Goulder, Michael, ed. *Incarnation and Myth: The Debate Continued.* Grand Rapids: Eerdmans, 1979.

Green, Michael. *The Truth of God Incarnate.* Grand Rapids: Eerdmans, 1977.

Gudmunsen, Chris. *Wittgenstein and Buddhism.* London: Macmillan, 1977.

Harnack, Adolf von. *What Is Christianity?* Translated by T. B. Sanders. New York: Putnam, 1908.

Heaton, Eric William. *The Old Testament Prophets.* Baltimore: Penguin, 1961.

Herrigel, Eugene. *Zen in the Art of Archery.* New York: Pantheon, 1953.

Hick, John. *The Metaphor of Incarnation.* London: John Knox, 2005.

———, ed. *The Myth of God Incarnate.* Philadelphia: Westminster, 1977.

———. "On Conflicting Truth Claims." *Religious Studies* 19 (1983) 485–91.

———. "On Grading Religions." *Religious Studies* 17 (1981) 451–67.

———. *Philosophy of Religion.* 1st and 2nd eds. Englewood Cliffs, NJ: Prentice-Hall, 1963 and 1973.

*Hymns of the Rig Veda.* Translated by Ralph Griffeth. Delhi: Motilal Banarsidass, 1973.

Kee, Howard Clark. *Jesus in History: An Approach to the Study of the Gospels.* New York: Harcourt, Brace, 1970.

Kee, Howard Clark, and Franklin W. Young. *Understanding the New Testament.* Englewood Cliffs, NJ: Prentice-Hall, 1957.

Kloppenborg, John S. *Q, the Earliest Gospel: An Introduction to the Earliest Sayings and Stories of Jesus.* Louisville: John Knox, 2008.

Kohlberg, Lawrence. *Essays on Moral Development.* Vol. 2, *The Psychology of Moral Development.* San Francisco: Harper & Row, 1984

———. "Stages of Moral Development as a basis of Moral Education." Chap. 1 of *Moral Education: Interdisciplinary Approaches*, edited by C. M. Beck et al. Toronto: Toronto University Press, 1971.

# Bibliography

*Large Sutra on Perfect Wisdom*. Translated by Edward Conze. Berkeley: University of California Press, 1975.

Lindbeck, George. *The Nature of Doctrine: Religion and Theology Is a Postliberal Age.* Philadelphia: Westminster, 1984.

Minus, Paul M. *Walter Rauschenbusch: American Reformer.* New York: Macmillan, 1988.

Moore, Edward. "Neo-Platonism." *Internet Encyclopedia of Philosophy.* http://www.iep.utm.edu/neoplato.

Mowrer, O. Hobart. *The Crisis in Psychiatry and Religion.* Princeton, NJ: Van Nostrand, 1966.

Niebuhr, Reinhold. *Moral Man and Immoral Society: A Study in Ethics and Politics.* New York: Scribner, 1960.

Prothero, Stephen. *God Is Not One.* New York: HarperOne, 1910.

Rauschenbusch, Walter. *Christianity and the Social Crisis.* New York: Macmillan, 1907.

———. *Christianity and the Social Crisis in the 21st Century.* Edited by Paul Rauschenbusch. New York: HarperCollins, 2007.

———. *The Social Principles of Jesus.* New York: Woman's, 1917.

———. *A Theology for the Social Gospel.* New York: MacMillan, 1918.

———. "Walter Rauschenbusch: Champion of the Social Gospel" *Christianity Today.com.* Posted August 8, 2008. http://www.christianitytoday.com/ch/131christians/activists/rauschenbusch.html.

Rioch, D. M. "Recollections of Harry Stack Sullivan and of the Development of His Interpersonal Psychiatry." *Psychiatry* 48 (1985) 141–58.

Ritschl, Albrecht. *A Critical History of the Christian Doctrine of Justification and Reconciliation.* Translated by H. R. Mackintosh and A. B. Macaulay. Clifton, NJ: Reference Book Publishers, 1966. Originally *Die Geschichte der Lehre.* Bonn, 1870.

Robinson, Richard H., and Willard L. Johnson. *The Buddhist Religion: A Historical Introduction.* 2nd ed. Encino, CA: Dickenson, 1977.

Rogers, Jack, and Donald McKim. *The Authority and Interpretation of Scripture: An Historical Approach.* New York: Harper & Row, 1979.

Ryle, Gilbert. *The Concept of Mind.* New York: Barnes & Noble, 1949.

Sasaki, Ruth Fuller. "Zen: A Method of Religious Awakening." Chap. 2 of *The World of Zen: An East-West Anthology*, by Nancy Wilson Ross. New York: Vintage, 1960.

Schleiermacher, Friedrich. *The Christian Faith.* Vol. 1. New York: Harper & Row, 1963.

———. *On Religion: Speeches to Its Cultured Despisers.* New York: Harper & Row, 1958.

Schweitzer, Albert. *The Quest of the Historical Jesus.* London: Black, 1910.

Sharpe, Dores Robinson. *Walter Rauschenbusch.* New York: MacMillan, 1942.

Spock, Benjamin. *The Common Sense Book of Baby and Child Care.* New York: Pocket, 1945.

Strong, Augustus Hopkins. *Systematic Theology: Designed for Theological Students.* Philadelphia: Judson, 1907.

SUSPS (Support US Population Stabilization). "Population Numbers, Projections, Graphs and Data." http://www.susps.org/overview/numbers.html.

Suzuki, Daisetz Teitaro. *Zen Buddhism: Selected Writings.* Edited by William Barrett. Garden City: Doubleday, 1956.

Tillich, Paul. *Systematic Theology.* Vols. 1–3. Chicago: University of Chicago Press, 1951–1963.

Toulmin, Stephen, et al. *Metaphysical Beliefs: Three Essays.* London: SCM, 1957.

*The Upanishads.* Translated by Juan Mascaro. London: Penguin, 1965.

# BIBLIOGRAPHY

Watts, Alan. *This Is It, and Other Essays on Zen and Spiritual Experience.* New York: Vintage, 1960.

———. *The Way of Zen.* New York: Pantheon, 1957.

Wellhausen, Julius. *Prolegomena to the History of Ancient Israel.* Translated by Allen Menzies and J. Sutherland Black. New York: Meridian, 1961.

West, James King. *Introduction to the Old Testament.* 2nd ed. New York: Macmillan, 1981.

Wittgenstein, Ludwig. *Blue and Brown Books.* Oxford: Blackwell, 1958.

———. *Lectures and Conversations on Aesthetics, Psychology, and Religious Belief.* Edited by Cyril Barret. Berkeley: University of California Press, 1967.

———. *On Certainty.* Edited by G. E. Anscombe and G. H. von Wright. New York: Harper & Row, 1972.

———. *Philosophical Investigations.* Translated by G. E. M. Anscombe. New York: Macmillan, 1955.